Trading
Dead-End
Relationships
for
Lasting
Love

Other Books by Willard F. Harley, Jr.

Fall in Love, Stay in Love

His Needs, Her Needs

His Needs, Her Needs for Parents

Love Busters

Five Steps to Romantic Love

I Cherish You

Your Love and Marriage

Surviving an Affair

The Four Gifts of Love

Give and Take

Trading Dead-End Relationships

for

Lasting Love

Willard F. Harley, Jr.

SPIRE

© 2002 by Willard F. Harley, Jr.

Published by Revell
a division of Baker Publishing Group
P.O. Box 6287, Grand Rapids, MI 49516-6287
www.revellbooks.com

Spire edition published 2011
ISBN 978-0-8007-8750-9

Originally published in 2002 under the title *Buyers, Renters & Freeloaders*

11   12   13   14   15   16   17   7   6   5   4   3   2   1

Contents

Contents

1

Looking for Lasting Love?

Have you ever been in love? If so, you know how great it feels to love and be loved by someone. When a romantic relationship is on track, you never want it to end. But, as you've probably noticed, it's hard to keep one on track. After starting out as terrific, your romantic relationships may have turned terrible or even terrifying, leaving you wondering what happened. If that's been your experience, you are not alone—most romantic relationships end up that way.

You've probably asked yourself the question, "Why? What makes my romantic relationships go from great to gone?" You may think that you just haven't found the right match yet, and that it's only a matter of time before the right one comes along. But I have another explanation, one that has helped keep thousands of romantic relationships on track—for life.

If you've come to a point where you're tired of revolving-door romance and want to create one romantic relationship that remains passionate and fulfilling for the rest of your life, this book is definitely for you. But even if you're not quite to that point, this book will help you understand the ups and

> *If you're tired of revolving-door romance,*
> *this book is definitely for you.*

downs of your current romantic relationship and help you accurately predict its future.

What's So Great about Romantic Relationships?

Let's define the most important term used in this book—romantic relationship. *A romantic relationship consists of two people in love who meet each other's emotional needs for intimacy.* My definition is admittedly narrow. Some people may believe they are in a romantic relationship, yet they are not in love with each other. Others may feel that a romantic relationship doesn't have to meet their emotional needs for intimacy. But from my perspective, people are not in a truly romantic relationship unless they are in love and meet each other's needs for intimacy.

Intimate needs are among the most important emotional needs we have in life. Affection, intimate conversation, sexual fulfillment, and admiration are just a few examples of these important needs. We cannot meet any of them by ourselves—they can only be met by someone else. And not by just anyone else. Only someone we love and who loves us can meet these needs in a way that is completely fulfilling. In other words,

---

Romantic Relationship

Two people in love who meet each other's emotional needs for intimacy.

8

we're wired to be in a romantic relationship. And when we are not, we feel that something's missing. That's why we find a romantic relationship so compelling—we need it.

Over the years I've written several books that explain how intimate emotional needs should be met in a romantic re-

We're wired to be in a romantic relationship.

lationship. The most popular of these books is *His Needs, Her Needs*, where I show couples how they can identify each other's intimate needs and then become experts at meeting them. If you're not sure how to meet someone's intimate emotional needs in a romantic relationship, you will find that book valuable reading.

In this book, however, I will assume that you already know how to meet emotional needs in a relationship with someone you love who also loves you. What still may be a mystery to you, though, is how to keep a great romantic relationship from turning into a disaster. If you could figure that out, your revolving-door romances would finally end. You could stop wasting your time and energy replacing one disappointing relationship with another. You'd finally have one that would last a lifetime.

Romance Is a Science

I've been married to my wife, Joyce, for forty years, and our love for each other is as strong and passionate today as it was when we first married. In the beginning, I really didn't know what made our relationship work so well. I had to spend a few years counseling those whose relationships were failing before I was able to clearly see what Joyce and I did (and still do) that made and kept us such passionate lovers.

Now, as I look back on the rocky beginning of our dating relationship, it all makes sense to me. But back then, my relationships with Joyce and everyone else I dated seemed like a frightening roller-coaster ride where I had no control. Dumb luck seemed to rule. How else could someone be crazy about me one day and loathe me the next? And how could I be crazy about someone for a while, only to become disinterested eventually? It seemed like I and the women I dated were the victims of magical spells.

But it wasn't magic. What made my dating experiences sensational one day and boring the next was scientifically predictable. It had to do with the quality of care I gave the women I dated and the care they showed me in return.

People show care for each other in a romantic relationship by meeting each other's intimate emotional needs. But a romantic relationship rarely begins with much of an effort to

What made my dating experiences
sensational one day and boring the
next was scientifically predictable.

meet intimate needs. In fact it usually begins with little or no effort at all. That's why so many romantic relationships have trouble getting out of the starting blocks. Did you (or do you) look forward to first dates? I didn't. That's because there's such a high likelihood that the care you give each other on that date will be mutually disappointing. You are both shopping around, and rejection is almost a certainty. One or both of you are likely to find the other lacking.

If a relationship does survive the initial introduction, and neither person does any rejecting, they often move on to a tentative willingness to provide mutual care—as long as the relationship is mutually advantageous. It is in this intermediate stage of creating a romantic relationship that two people can fall in love with each other because their care hits the mark. Rejection can still take place—it did for Joyce and me—but the couple knows better how to avoid it.

Finally, if two people who are in love decide to commit their care to each other exclusively and permanently, they have completed their creation of a romantic relationship that will last a lifetime. This highest level of care guarantees their love for each other for life. There are millions of fulfilling marriages that prove it, mine included.

I've written this book to help you understand the three levels of care I have just described. They have almost everything to do with the success and failure of your romantic

The highest level of care guarantees a couple's love for each other for life.

relationships. I call those who operate under these levels of care Buyers, Renters, and Freeloaders. Each differs from the others in several important ways that I'll explain in the next few chapters, but their main difference is the quality of care they are willing to provide to make a relationship mutually fulfilling.

A *Freeloader* is unwilling to put much effort into the care of his or her partner in a romantic relationship. He or she does only what comes naturally and expects only what comes naturally. It's like a person who tries to live in a house without paying rent or doing anything to improve it unless the person is in the mood to do so.

A *Renter* is willing to provide limited care as long as it's in his or her best interest. The romantic relationship is considered tentative, so the care is viewed as short-term. It's like a person who rents a house and is willing to stay as long as the conditions seem fair, or until he or she finds something better. The person is willing to pay reasonable rent and keep the house clean but is not willing to make repairs or improvements. It's the landlord's job to keep the place attractive enough for the renter to stay and continue paying rent.

A *Buyer* is willing to demonstrate an extraordinary sense of care by making permanent changes in his or her own behavior and lifestyle to make the romantic relationship mutually fulfilling. Solutions to problems are long-term solutions and must work well for both partners because the romantic relationship is viewed as exclusive and permanent. It's like a person who buys a house for life with a willingness to make repairs that accommodate changing needs — painting the walls, installing new carpet, replacing the roof, and even doing some remodeling — so that it can be comfortable and useful.

As I mentioned, it's not uncommon for most happily married couples to have worked their way up from Freeloaders to Renters and finally to Buyers. I know that's how my wife, Joyce, and I developed our relationship. There's nothing wrong with being a Freeloader, when first trying to create a romantic relationship, or a Renter, as the relationship is developing. The problem arises when partners do not eventually become Buyers. As I will show you, Freeloaders and Renters cannot create a lasting romantic relationship, and, as a result, they make very disappointing marriage partners because the romantic part of their relationship disappears. Only Buyers can create the permanent romantic relationship that keeps marriage passionate and mutually fulfilling.

The unspoken agreements of care between a man and a woman influence the course of their romantic relationship, both positively and negatively. Relationships thrive on mutual care, and they die when that care is not forthcoming. By the time you finish reading this book, you will be able to identify the agreements of care that characterize your present relation-

This book will help you predict with near certainty the future of your romantic relationship.

ship, and you will be able to predict with near certainty the future of your relationship—unless your agreement changes. You'll also learn how you can try out the Buyer's agreement without actually becoming a Buyer. That way you can see for yourself why it will guarantee the success of your relationship and why the Renter's and Freeloader's agreements will cause it to fail.

Finding a fulfilling and permanent romantic relationship is one of life's greatest achievements. But failure to find such a relationship can be one of life's greatest frustrations. If you have almost given up hope of finding a romantic relationship that doesn't end in disappointment, don't despair. This book will provide the formula you need to make your current or next romantic relationship last a lifetime.

PART 1

Buyers, Renters, and Freeloaders— What Are They?

2

What You See Is What You Get

The Freeloader's Agreement

Frank,

Before we go any further, I want you to understand that I am really past complexities now. I don't want to work at making love work. It must never be hard or it is just not worth it. I do what I do because I like to do it and I never expect anything in return.

I will never again be the crutch for someone else. I won't be drained by someone else's needs, someone who is too crippled in his own emotions to be able to give me what it is I need or deserve too.

I am not sure what it is that you want from me, Frank. But I am happier now in my

```
life than I have ever been. I have finally
given myself permission to enjoy life and
to love me, and I have no desire to take
myself on a backward spiral ever again.
```

```
Brenda
```

Sounds harsh, doesn't it? Not all Freeloaders state their position as bluntly as Brenda did to Frank. In fact few do. But Brenda's letter, which was sent to Frank in the beginning of their dating relationship, does accurately describe some of the attitudes all Freeloaders share.

Brenda has very limited objectives for a romantic relationship and is only willing to give and receive care if it comes almost effortlessly. She obviously has issues that have an impact on her attitude. But even if her past relationships had not been so unpleasant, she may have taken the same position in the beginning of her relationship with Frank.

Behind every romantic relationship, there is an agreement between the partners. Sometimes it is unspoken and poorly understood. But sometimes it is as clear as Brenda's letter

> *Behind every romantic relationship, there is an agreement between the partners.*

to Frank. The ball is now in his court as to whether he will accept or try to modify her agreement. If he wants to create a romantic relationship with her on her terms, it will develop as a Freeloader's relationship.

As I mentioned earlier, a Freeloader is like someone who lives in a house without paying rent or doing anything to maintain or improve it unless he or she feels like it. This willingness to provide very limited care in a romantic relationship is usually based on certain beliefs that make it seem

---

A Freeloader's Creed

- Romantic relationships shouldn't be work.
- Love me as I am or not at all.
- Bargaining is for businessmen, not lovers.

---

reasonable. These are some of the beliefs that support the Freeloader's agreement:

1. There are romantic relationships that are right for me and those that are wrong for me. Those that are right for me make me happy without my having to put much effort into making my partner happy. He or she should be happy with what I do that comes almost effortlessly for me. But romantic relationships that are wrong for me require me to do things that do not come naturally.

2. If I am in a romantic relationship with someone who criticizes me, it is a sign that the relationship is wrong for me. It's a mistake for me to change my behavior to accommodate a critical partner, because I'm only prolonging a relationship that isn't meant to be.

3. A romantic relationship that is right for me requires unconditional care and acceptance. If my partner expects me to do something in return for what he or she has done for me, it's a sign that the relationship is not based on unconditional care and, as such, is wrong for me. It's a mistake to try to change my behavior to make a relationship seem fair to my partner, because I should be unconditionally accepted for who I am and what I do.

People who use the Freeloader's agreement are not usually selfish misfits. In fact most of us have been in relationships with Freeloaders who have turned out to do just fine in life. And we ourselves have been Freeloaders at some time in our life.

I began dating when I was fifteen. Prior to that, I had girlfriends but never went on any official dates with any of them. My first real date was with Joyce, the girl who eventually became my wife. My sister, who was her best friend, told me that Joyce would go out with me if I asked, so I asked.

Between the ages of fifteen and seventeen, I was a Freeloader. I expected the girl I dated to put up with whatever I had in mind, and Joyce was my first test case. If she was right for me, I figured, she would want to be with me regardless of what we did. So I didn't always tell her what we would be doing when I picked her up for a date, and I prided myself on getting through an evening without having to spend much money. I also expected her to drop any plans she might have had for the evening if I were to decide to go out. So Joyce eventually did what you'd expect—she broke up with me.

I had been taking Joyce for granted, and she didn't like it. If I wanted to date her again, I would have to change my ways. So when we finally got back together, I became a much

There is something to be said for the Freeloader's approach, especially at the beginning of a relationship.

more thoughtful person. I became a Renter. And that helped improve our relationship considerably.

Now despite the fact that my Freeloading style didn't work very well during my early days of dating, there is something to be said for the Freeloader's approach, especially at the beginning of a relationship. It has to do with the fact that some men and women have a certain "chemistry" with each other, and others do not. There really is something to the idea of being right or wrong for each other.

The Beauty Contest

I was a psychology professor teaching graduate and under-graduate level courses for ten years, and during that time I taught many different courses. But the one I most enjoyed teaching was Introduction to Psychology, because it offered me an opportunity to present my discipline as the sumptuous buffet of fascinating topics that it is.

During each class, I provided a demonstration to illustrate some aspect of the day's topic. And one day I offered the "beauty contest." A female volunteer was the judge, and five male volunteers were the contestants. The judge was connected to electrodes, and I measured her galvanic skin response (GSR), which was the change in her skin resistance to electrical current. You see, whenever any of us has an emotional reaction, it can be measured in our skin resistance, which becomes lower. Then, as we recover our composure, our skin resistance rises again.

In my beauty contest, I wanted to know which of our five contestants would give our judge the biggest and most consistent emotional buzz. In other words, which one would she find most emotionally attractive? One way to discover the answer was to measure her GSR for each contestant.

Each of the five male volunteers stood in front of the judge for about thirty seconds. He was not to say or do anything. The meter that measured her skin resistance was visible to the class, and they recorded the change, but they were not to react to the measurement. Then our female judge would have about thirty seconds to recover before the next contestant would have a chance to impress her.

We went through the process three times, changing the order of appearance each time. After the contest was over, the class had an opportunity to ask the judge whether her change in skin resistance was a true indicator of her attraction to the winner. Every time I offered this demonstration, the judge would admit that the contest winner was indeed the one she liked the most. After the contest was over, I suggested that

We had witnessed scientific evidence for "chemistry."

the winner take the judge out on a date at least once, because we had witnessed scientific evidence for "chemistry."

I conducted a more time-consuming version of the same demonstration in my lab. In that experiment, I had three different female judges react to the same five men. I found that each time I conducted this experiment, the three women did not react the same way to the five men. The winner for one judge would tend to be different for another judge. And even the level of reaction would be different. One man would elicit no reaction at all for one of the judges but would cause the needle to go off the meter for another.

My beauty contest demonstrated a phenomenon that we all know to be true—some people find us more attractive than others. It also demonstrated something else that most of us know—beauty is in the eye of the beholder. What is ho-hum to one person is wow! to another.

Of course, this phenomenon applies not only to those who find us attractive but also to those who find us unattractive. In other words, there are those who like us instinctively, and there are also those who dislike us instinctively, at least when they first get to know us.

Lovers, Likers, Dislikers, and Haters

With these instincts in mind, I've found it useful to classify all of humanity into four groups — the Lovers, the Likers, the Dislikers, and the Haters.

The Lovers are those who like just about everything there is about you. They like the way you look, the way you talk, the way you think, and the way you react to things. And the more they get to know you, the more attracted they tend to become.

Likers are also attracted to you, but they notice a few flies in the ointment. If they think it is rude to be critical, you may never know about their negative reactions. But if they are honest, their occasional suggestions for your improvement will slip out.

If you have ever spoken with someone who tends to be very critical of you, you are probably talking with a Disliker. These people find most of what you are and do to be substandard, but they are charitable enough to give you a chance to meet their standards. It is very difficult for these people to avoid being judgmental, because so much of what you do irritates them.

Then there are the Haters. These are people who don't like anything about you. From their perspective, you are hopelessly unappealing. You rarely hear any criticism from this group

---

Words Say It All

- Lover—"I love every little thing about you!"
- Liker—"You're okay."
- Disliker—"If only . . . you could really go places."
- Hater—(You hear nothing because these folks don't hang around!)

23

because they cannot stand to be around you long enough to criticize you. Besides, from their perspective there is nothing you can do to redeem yourself.

Of course, your Lovers, Likers, Dislikers, and Haters are different from mine. Each of us has our own unique grouping of all humanity because people react to each one of us differently.

My experience as a professor brought me face to face with some of *my* Lovers, Likers, Dislikers, and Haters. I had a captive audience and I encouraged them to anonymously critique my teaching. Some students thought I was their best teacher and others gave me an above average rating. But some thought I needed to improve a great deal to meet their standards, and

The more people I get to know, the more impressed I am with how some are meant to be with others.

a few thought I should give up teaching entirely and get into some other career where I wouldn't annoy so many people.

What intrigued me about these evaluations was that I was doing the same things when I was with all four types of students. But they reacted differently. I was perfectly suited to teach some of these students, while for others I was their worst nightmare.

The more people I get to know, the more impressed I am with how some are meant to be with others. Those I find delightful are often considered boring by others I know. And those I find downright disgusting have friends who find them entertaining.

This insight has made me very reluctant to try to change people or even suggest that they change. After all, what right do I have to tell people that they should change their behavior to suit me when there are thousands of people who would find their behavior perfect?

Freeloaders Search for Their Lovers

The fact that there are some people who instinctively like me and others who instinctively dislike me led me to my early dating strategy. When I asked a girl out, I went to very little trouble to entertain her. If she did not like my style, I simply concluded we were not right for each other. There wasn't enough chemistry. I was a Freeloader when it came to dating because I expected to be accepted unconditionally and went to little or no trouble to accommodate the girls I dated, doing for them only what came naturally.

Whenever I called Joyce for a date, she would respond with an enthusiastic "I'd love to." That's what I wanted to hear, and it encouraged me to continue my Freeloading ways, right up to the day she broke up with me.

Fortunately for Joyce, and for me, she was ultimately unwilling to put up with my Freeloading approach to dating. While she was definitely a Lover, because there was so much she liked about me, my approach to dating almost ruined it all. She knew I was as attracted to her as she was to me, but I didn't seem to care for her. All I cared about was myself. So she broke up with me.

But what about chemistry? Wasn't that enough? Apparently not. The chemistry Joyce had for me wasn't enough to overcome my thoughtlessness. As it turns out, those who are our Lovers don't remain Lovers if we don't treat them right. We can run them off when we behave in an obnoxious way. That's why Freeloaders usually have very few long-term•

relationships. They find Lovers who have a natural attraction to them and then wreck it all by being thoughtless.

When Joyce broke up with me for the first time, I was devastated. There was no warning. After a very enjoyable

Our Lovers don't remain our Lovers

if we don't treat them right.

evening with her, she announced at the door that she would not be dating me any longer.

Of course, my Freeloading philosophy had a ready response to her rejection. We were not right for each other, so I should never date her again. After all, why try to force something that's just not meant to be? But in the days and weeks that followed, every time I saw her, I seemed to die inside. I was in love.

Love has a way of changing our philosophy of life, and that was certainly true in my relationship with Joyce. Eventually I decided that if I ever got a chance to date Joyce again, I would try to be more considerate of her feelings. I had been converted into a Renter.

3

I'll Do Anything to Make You Happy . . . for a While

The Renter's Agreement

For about five years I was the proud owner of a dating service. I called it Help Meet. There were about a thousand members, and my goal was to help them meet and eventually marry each other. Each member completed several questionnaires to help identify what it was they were looking for in a spouse and what they had to offer that person. Then I tried to match them according to their criteria and interests.

After each date, both members completed another questionnaire that evaluated their experience with each other. After collecting these evaluations for about six months, I was astonished to discover that almost everyone thought their dates were a waste of time. Although they were matched for values, lifestyle, and interests, when they actually got together, they didn't get along. All of them thought they were dating losers.

But hardly any of them thought that they were losers themselves. In fact they were usually insulted that I would try to match them with someone they considered so inferior. In other words, they clearly saw problems in their dates, but they didn't see any problems in themselves.

These evaluations were extremely helpful in figuring out why these people had been single so long. Remember what I said about Lovers, Likers, Dislikers, and Haters? Well, these people had developed their Freeloading ways to such perfection that they tended to chase their would-be Lovers away,

Instead of a date being a test of compatibility,

it became an opportunity to improve

their ability to care for others.

just as I had chased Joyce away at first. For some it took several dates to prove their rudeness, but others were able to accomplish it after just five minutes of conversation. The evaluations clearly showed that their Freeloading philosophy, and the insensitivity that accompanied it, needed to change.

So I began working with some of them individually to help them avoid leaving such a bad first impression. Instead of a date being a test of compatibility, it became an opportunity to improve their ability to care for others. I continued receiving evaluations, but now members used them as a way to discover their social weaknesses that needed improvement.

I encouraged each member to regard his or her very first date with someone as an opportunity to gather data on the subject of care. They were to try to discover what made the other person happy and what made the other person unhappy.

I suggested questions to ask regarding their date's most enjoyable memories and most dreadful experiences. The answers would help them learn what they could do to make the person happy and avoid making the person unhappy. After the first date, they would try to put into practice what they had learned about caring for that person.

For some members of my dating service, Freeloading had become such a habit that they needed some basic training before I could trust them with a first date. I had them practice conversational etiquette—how to balance conversation so that one person doesn't do all the talking or listening and how to look at the other person when conversing. They learned not to interrupt, not to be argumentative, and not to be disrespectful.

I taught other members how to become more physically attractive for a first date. They lost weight. They dressed bet-

The skills they learned didn't change who they really were, but they did make them more visible and vibrant to their Lovers.

ter. They improved their hygiene. First impressions mean a great deal, even to Lovers.

And in some cases, I had to encourage members of my dating service to get a job before they had their first date. Unemployment is a huge turnoff to most Lovers.

In effect, I helped my dating service members learn the lessons I'd learned when Joyce rejected my Freeloading ways. The skills they learned didn't change who they really were, but they did make them more visible and vibrant to their Lovers. By becoming less argumentative, they were not hiding their inner feelings, but rather they were expressing them more constructively. And by losing weight, they were not changing their true identity, but rather they were presenting themselves as healthier and happier. I was converting my members from Freeloaders to Renters.

A Tentative Agreement

The Renter is willing to put more effort into caring for a partner in a romantic relationship than is a Freeloader. Freeloaders are willing to do only what comes naturally, but Renters are willing to improve their ability to care—as long as it is in their best interest to do so. It's like a person who is willing to pay whatever rent is necessary to live in the house of his or her choice, but reserves the right to leave if it is no longer suitable or affordable or if something better can be found. He or she agrees to keep the house clean but is not usually willing to make major repairs or improvements.

This agreement, to provide short-term care as long as it's worth the effort, is usually based on certain beliefs that make such an agreement reasonable. These are the beliefs that support the Renter's agreement:

1. Romantic relationships require a certain amount of give and take, but it's only right for me if what I take is worth what I give. Someone who is right for me today can be wrong for me tomorrow. The person may be what I need in one stage of my life but not what I need in another, so my romantic relationships should be considered temporary. If what I take isn't worth what I give, either my partner should give me more, or I should end the relationship to find someone who will give me what I need.

2. If I am in a romantic relationship with someone who criticizes me, it does not necessarily mean that my

---

A Renter's Creed

- Romantic relationships require care—but that's only okay if it's fair.
- I'll change for you if it's worth my while.
- I'll sacrifice for you if you sacrifice for me.

---

partner is wrong for me if I can make the necessary changes. But my change should be made only if what I get from my partner is worth the effort.

3. If I am in a romantic relationship and my partner expects me to sacrifice my own happiness to meet my partner's needs in return for what my partner has done for me, that's a reasonable expectation. And if I feel I am getting less than I deserve, it's reasonable for me to expect my partner to sacrifice some happiness for my fulfillment.

Renters do not believe that they should be cared for unconditionally as Freeloaders do. In fact they believe that they should match the care they receive in a romantic relationship with the care they provide in return. They regularly evaluate

Renters' willingness to sacrifice comes from their assumption that the relationship is temporary.

how fair their relationship is, making sure that the levels of effort and sacrifice are even. If Renters believe they are giving more than they are getting, they feel justified in demanding more for themselves to balance the scales. And when their demands are unmet, it often leads to fights.

Renters' willingness to sacrifice and expect sacrifice comes from their assumption that the relationship is temporary. They are not thinking about long-term solutions to problems but rather about short-term fixes. So their care for the other person is temporary. But even that is a big improvement over the lack of care shown by Freeloaders.

My dating service members became Renters when they decided to make an effort to care for those they dated. But their effort was short-term—one date at a time. Some gave up after a few unrewarded attempts to be caring. To them the effort just wasn't worth it. Others, who felt that the care they received from their date equaled or surpassed the care they gave, kept dating the person.

My newly converted Renters were willing to be more caring so that they could *attract* better candidates for marriage. But in the process, they also *became* better candidates for marriage. Members who followed my plan saw an astonishing rise in dating opportunities and, in some cases, marriage proposals. Their improved ability to demonstrate their care and thoughtfulness, even though it was only tentative, was all it took to attract Lovers who wanted to share life with them. As you would expect, the number of marriages resulting from my dating service increased substantially.

What I said earlier about Lovers, Likers, Dislikers, and Haters still held true with my members. The purpose of the service was not to make them attractive to everyone, but rather to help them discover their natural Lovers. And they could do that much more effectively when the distraction of their thoughtless behavior was eliminated. As Freeloaders, their true value to others was hidden away. But as Renters, they were able to demonstrate their ability to care in ways that had been masked by their Freeloading attitudes and habits. With those distractions eliminated, their Lovers saw them for who they really were.

Personal Characteristics That Match for Compatibility

My dating service members needed to do more than find their Lovers—those who were especially attracted to them. They also had to find those for whom they were Lovers—those to whom they felt a special attraction. I didn't want them to settle for Likers, and I certainly didn't want them to end up with Dislikers. So to help them find their Lover-Lover matches, I had to give them plenty of dating opportunities that maximized their chances of discovering that combination.

My rule of thumb was to introduce each member to thirty new people a year, and from that group of thirty, most people

> *My rule of thumb was to introduce each member to thirty new people a year.*

were able to find their perfect match. But to make that group of thirty likely to contain the perfect match, I had each member complete a questionnaire that helped screen out those who were unlikely to be their Lovers.

Just as I was able to teach members to improve their appearance, conversational skills, and even their ability to earn a living, I could also teach them other important skills that would enhance their ability to provide care in a romantic relationship. But there were five characteristics that made such instruction either easy or difficult, depending on who their partner happened to be. So my questionnaire focused special attention on those characteristics. When a couple was matched in these areas, whatever instruction they would need about meeting each other's intimate emotional needs would be relatively easy to provide.

1. Intelligence

You and your partner should be roughly equivalent in intelligence. Without having to take an IQ test, you can usually figure out whether this is so by comparing grades in school, although men can be notorious underachievers in high school. College grades, ACT scores, and SAT scores are usually a much better measure of intelligence for both men and women if you have access to any of these records.

The quality of your conversation is another good indicator of compatible intelligence. Those whom you find stimulating to talk to are usually in your league intellectually. But if there is a large intelligence gap between you, both of you will tend to be bored by your conversation. The one with the higher IQ will find the conversation to be superficial, and the one with the lower IQ won't be able to keep up. There is also a tendency of someone with a higher IQ to disrespect the judgments of the one with the lower IQ, and that's an absolute relationship killer. Respect is essential in romantic relationships regardless of the quality of an opinion.

If you both enjoy talking to each other for hours at a time and you tend to respect each other's ideas and the way they are expressed, you probably pass the IQ test.

2. Energy

You and your partner should be roughly equivalent to each other in energy. Energy is an important determiner of compatibility because so many of your lifestyle predispositions depend on your energy level. Leisure time activities and sexual interest are particularly sensitive to the amount of energy you have. People high in energy enjoy activities that burn that energy, even after work, while those with low energy levels would find such activities exhausting. In the case of sex, the more energy a person has, the more sex he or she tends to need. Since leisure activities and sex are two of the best ways to enjoy time together after marriage, incompatibility in these areas can make it very difficult for a couple to create a fulfilling and permanent romantic relationship.

If one of you lies around watching television while the other scurries about and can't sit still, you're probably a bad match. But if you find that you enjoy activities that require the same amount of energy from both of you, you probably pass the energy test.

3. Social Interest

If one of you is socially outgoing and the other is shy, you'll have a hard time planning social activities. In romantic relationships between extroverts and introverts, the area of mutual social comfort is very narrow. The extrovert will not be able to get to know as many people as he or she would like because the introvert hates meeting new people. And the introvert will be constantly challenged to tread into the terrifying waters of introductions. It's important for those in a romantic relationship to be together socially rather than go their separate ways (one goes to a party and the other stays home). So when social interests differ, a couple struggles to make their social lives enjoyable for both of them. It's much easier to simply have a partner with similar social interests.

If one of you has dozens of friends already but still wants more and the other has very few friends with no interest in adding to the list, I'd be concerned. However, if you have a similar reaction, either positive or negative, when you think about meeting people for the first time, you probably pass the social interest test.

4. Cultural Background

Culture determines a host of personal sensitivities that must be accommodated in a romantic relationship. Take Christmas, for example. In the American culture, Christmas is a big deal for most people. If you grew up in a family in which Christmas was celebrated with zeal every year, imagine discovering that your partner never celebrated it at all. The time and energy required to make Christmas a memorable occasion wouldn't be appreciated by your partner. And he or she would lack the background to help you make it memorable. Most celebrations, such as birthdays and Valentine's Day, are driven by culture. And when you have not been raised in a culture that appreciates these events, they seem like a lot of wasted energy.

Cultural background not only dictates sensitivities, but it also dictates certain skills. The celebration of cherished events is very difficult to pull off if you have not been trained in doing it well. But it's not just celebrations that require skill. The skills necessary to meet certain emotional needs can also be culturally driven. For example, in some cultures, outward displays of affection are discouraged, yet you may need that from your partner. To meet your emotional need, he or she must not only learn to do something that was never taught, but he or she must also go against cultural sensitivities.

Sometimes when two people are in love, they feel that they can overcome cultural barriers. But that's usually because their relationship has been rather brief, or they have had limited exposure to situations that magnify their cultural differences. They have not yet had to wrestle with some of the conflicts that culture imposes on them. Don't underestimate the impact of cultural differences on a romantic relationship, particularly after children arrive.

5. *Values*

Moral values usually dictate how we behave. These are the spoken and unspoken rules that help us make decisions in life. If you and your partner have conflicts over moral values, creating a compatible lifestyle can be very difficult. Getting back to our Christmas example, it's a cultural difference that makes a spouse unskilled in knowing how to celebrate Christmas or appreciating its importance. But if you like to celebrate Christmas yet marry an Orthodox Jew, it's more than skill that will be a problem. Your spouse will probably be deeply offended by such a celebration. And that offense comes from moral convictions, not just cultural background.

A discussion of values is always a good idea on a date, because if you find that your values are very divergent, you know it will be difficult for you to agree on a lifestyle that you both feel comfortable sharing. A question I often ask engaged couples is, "Would you be willing to give up your religion or other values to please your partner?" That question gets right to the core of the importance of a person's values in his or her life. Is there some belief that is so important to you that you would be willing to let your partner suffer rather than give it up? If so, you should be certain that your partner shares the same belief before he or she becomes your spouse.

How Does Your Relationship Rate?

How well are you and your partner matched in these five areas?

√ Intelligence

√ Energy

√ Social Interest

√ Cultural Background

√ Values

Compatibility Can Be Learned

If you and your partner are very different in any of these five characteristics, it will be difficult to provide the quality of care that is needed in a romantic relationship. But it *is* possible for you to learn how to meet each other's emotional needs even when these differences exist. I've taught many couples how to do it. It's just much easier to do when you're matched.

But sometimes it's tempting to deliberately choose a partner who differs from you in one or more of these five characteristics. In fact, many well-meaning marriage advisors encourage it. They feel that what makes a romantic relationship vibrant is the differences between partners. To be in a relationship with someone like yourself is boring, they say. That may be true for some differences, such as masculinity and femininity.

Try to match yourself with someone who is compatible with you in these five areas.

I, for one, find Joyce to be very attractive because she is so feminine, which makes us very different from each other. But if we had been a mismatch in any of the five characteristics that I've just mentioned, our romantic relationship would have been much more difficult than it has been. Partners can enhance their romantic relationships with differences in many of their personal characteristics. But to differ on any one of the five my questionnaire measures usually means considerable training to adjust for those differences.

So if you are not yet married, try to match yourself with someone who is compatible with you in these five areas. That way, you will have a much easier time creating the kind of care for each other that will make your relationship thrive.

Doom for a Romantic Relationship

When I converted my dating service members from Freeloaders into Renters, I helped them create tentative romantic relationships. And there was nothing wrong with the short-term objectives they had at that stage in their search for a permanent relationship. In fact I regard the Renter's agreement as an essential stage in the development of any romantic relationship. But if that Renter's agreement lasts too long, the relationship can get very ugly. I'll explain why that happens further on in our discussion. But for now, I simply want you to know that the Renter's agreement will not usually sustain a romantic relationship.

The Renter's agreement *is* more effective than the Freeloader's agreement. Freeloaders are in a romantic relationship as long as they are in love and happen to be meeting some of each other's important emotional needs. But because they make no special effort to care for each other, their needs are not met consistently or effectively. And their thoughtlessness usually destroys their love for each other fairly soon after the relationship begins.

The romantic relationships of Renters have more staying power. Renters know they are together to meet each other's emotional needs, so they make a special effort to achieve that objective. In fact Renters rarely deny each other's requests

The Renter's agreement is an essential stage in the development of any romantic relationship.

to meet these needs. They do whatever it takes to make the relationship fulfilling for their partner—as long as it's fulfilling for themselves too. But Renters are always looking for something better, and their expectations of each other tend to increase the longer the relationship lasts. Eventually, instead of

39

giving each other anything that's desired, they begin limiting their care for each other, because they feel the other person is not meeting their standards. And they start making demands, showing disrespect, and becoming angry when they do not get what they think is fair. Eventually, almost all Renters' relationships become abusive. They do better than Freeloaders in a romantic relationship, but they cannot experience sustained fulfillment until they become Buyers.

A romantic relationship begins the day a couple in love starts meeting each other's important emotional needs, and it ends the day they stop meeting those needs. Renters usually do a great job meeting those emotional needs in the beginning

Renters do better than Freeloaders in a romantic relationship, but they cannot experience sustained fulfillment until they become Buyers.

of their relationship, but their willingness and commitment to continue meeting those needs drops off the longer the relationship lasts. So if a couple follows a Renter's agreement, their relationship will not be romantic very long.

People marry because they think they can sustain their romantic relationship for life. I certainly would not have married Joyce if I had thought that the romantic part of our relationship would end after we were married or as soon as we had children. The exclusive and permanent commitment to care that we made at the time of our marriage was not just a commitment to live together for life. It was a commitment to meet each other's intimate emotional needs for life. We agreed to do what it would take to have a permanent and exclusive romantic relationship.

The Freeloader's agreement would not have provided that outcome. We would have begun passing by each other like ships in the night if we had been Freeloaders. And the Renter's agreement would not have sustained our romantic relationship either. In fact it would have guaranteed an ugly end to our relationship. Only the Buyer's agreement was able to give us the permanent and exclusive romantic relationship that we promised each other.

4

We'll Be Lovers Till Death Do Us Part

The Buyer's Agreement

After Joyce broke up with me due to my insensitivity, I abandoned my Freeloading notion that I should be cared for unconditionally and decided that she was worth much more effort than I had given her earlier. No more unannounced and cheap dates. I began to treat her with a great deal more care because I didn't want to lose her—at least not just yet. As long as no one better came along, Joyce was worth treating with special care. I had become a Renter.

Joyce was a Renter too. She made it very clear to me that, although she liked me, she was also looking at other prospects. But when we were together, I was what she needed, and she was exactly what I needed.

The next time we broke up, it was more or less by mutual consent. She wanted to date other men and I wanted to date other women. We both let each other know that it didn't mean we wanted to lose each other. It just meant we had not made a permanent commitment. After all, we were Renters, and we wanted to try out a few other "houses."

I dated many other women while we were apart, but none compared with Joyce. Joyce was also disappointed with the men she dated, and eventually we started seeing each other again. Then one day, as we were on Sterns Wharf in Santa Barbara, I looked at her and remarked, "We should probably get married some day."

Joyce was taken by surprise. Was this a proposal? If so, it wasn't nearly good enough. Where was the ring? Where was the romantic setting? Where was the proposal itself? I had momentarily fallen back to my insensitive Freeloading ways.

But I quickly recovered my Renter's spirit and suggested that I make the proposal all over again. With help from Joyce, I bought a ring. Then we went to a romantic chapel, I got on my knee, and after the chapel bell rang twelve times, I asked her to marry me. She accepted, and the rest is history. She was nineteen and I was twenty.

Until the moment of our marriage, both Joyce and I were Renters. In fact, during our engagement, Joyce actually dated another guy as a last fling. I was somewhat concerned that she might do the same after we were married, but she assured me that once her vows were said, she would not so much as look at another guy. Well, she did look, but for the past forty years, I have been her exclusive romantic partner. When we married, we made the decision to become Buyers.

A *Buyer* is committed to providing exclusive and permanent care in a romantic relationship and makes decisions that reflect long-term consideration of the other person's feelings and interests. Since the relationship is for life, he or she is willing to permanently change behavior to make the relationship romantic and successful.

This agreement to provide care permanently is usually based on certain beliefs that make such an agreement

When we married, we made the

decision to become Buyers.

reasonable. These are the beliefs that support the Buyer's agreement:

1. We are in this romantic relationship for life, so our decisions must make both of us happy and fulfilled. We will provide each other consistent and effective care to make our relationship romantic and successful. When either of us finds our important emotional needs changing, we will change our habits and lifestyle to accommodate each other so that our relationship can be fulfilling to both of us throughout life.

2. If either of us is critical of the other, it indicates that an adjustment of habits and lifestyle is required until the change meets the standards set by the critic. If one of us has a problem with some aspect of the relationship, we will work together to find a solution that we can both permanently adopt.

3. The solution to every problem in our romantic relationship should be a long-term solution that satisfies both of us. Short-term sacrifice of one partner may be inevitable to create new habits or lifestyle changes to accommodate the other, but in the end, unless both of us are happy with the change, it cannot be considered an adequate solution. So long-term sacrifice should not

---

A Buyer's Creed

- Romantic relationships require consistent and effective mutual care.
- We'll adjust to each other as often as necessary.
- Wanted: long-term solutions that make us both happy, not short-term fixes that work for one and not the other.

---

be tolerated by either of us. The goal of our relationship is for both of us to be happy and fulfilled with every aspect of the relationship. As such, each of us must do everything with the other partner's interests and feelings in mind.

Imagine for a moment what it would take for two people to have a romantic relationship for life. Obviously their decisions should take each other's interests and feelings into account so that they create a lifestyle that would make them both happy. And they should continue to meet each other's emotional needs just as they did when getting into the romantic relationship in the first place, even if those needs change.

These goals are long-term goals. They require careful planning and execution, with a willingness to abandon lifestyle habits that are not mutually advantageous. They do not allow long-term sacrifice of one for the benefit of the other. Instead, they stress win-win solutions to all problems, because those are the best long-term solutions.

Sacrifice Doesn't Work for Long

If you really care about your partner, you won't encourage him or her to suffer if it's only on your behalf. Not even once. That's because care, by definition, is your willingness and ability to make your partner happy and avoid making him or her unhappy. When you expect your partner to suffer so you can have what you want, you are not caring anymore. You are lapsing into selfishness, as we all do from time to time, and it can have devastating consequences for a romantic relationship.

There is a place for sacrifice in romantic relationships when a long-term objective may require one or both partners to sacrifice short-term. But even short-term sacrifice for long-term

If you really care about your partner,
you won't encourage him or her to suffer
on your behalf—not even once.

objectives is a risky business, and you must think it through carefully if it is to have a mutually beneficial outcome.

For example, if a married couple decides to sell their home and move to a more desirable home, both spouses will sacrifice their happiness during the move. If the sacrifice is mutually agreed on and provides a clear benefit for both spouses, the sacrifice enhances the relationship. But if one partner forces the other to sacrifice, or even if one partner willingly sacrifices his or her own interests for the other's benefit, the long-term results can be disastrous.

As another example, consider a recreational activity that is unpleasant for one partner. In an effort to meet the other partner's need for recreational companionship, the reluctant partner sacrifices his or her happiness as an act of generosity. The result is that the particular activity becomes associated with unhappiness for that partner and leads to an aversive reaction. The sacrifice, which is intended to be short-term, ends up having long-term consequences. Instead of becoming a fulfilling recreational companion, the partner making the sacrifice grows to hate the particular recreation and gets sick whenever he or she thinks about it. In the end, short-term sacrifice can limit or even eliminate the long-term ability of the relationship to meet emotional needs.

If a couple wants a fulfilling relationship, neither must sacrifice for the other. Instead, their recreational activities

---

If a couple wants a fulfilling relationship,

neither must sacrifice for the other.

---

must be mutually enjoyable, or they will eventually come to an end. That's the way it is for everything else a couple wants from each other as well. Unless they meet each other's needs with mutual enjoyment, those needs won't be met long-term.

Lapses into selfishness are usually tolerated in short-term relationships guided by the Renter's agreement. That's because sacrifice is not just expected—it's usually demanded. And the demands of Renters are backed up by their threat of leaving. *If you don't accommodate me, I will end my relationship with you*, is a common theme.

Unfortunately, leaving is not a Renter's only threat. When a demand is not met, a Renter feels justified in becoming verbally or even physically abusive to get what he or she feels is fair. That's why fights are so common in Renters' relationships.

But Renters can escape. Short-term sacrifice, and even abuse, doesn't trap Renters because they can always leave each other. They can move out if the house becomes unlivable. It's a different story, though, when a couple who is committed to an exclusive and permanent relationship requires sacrifice of each other. Their demand for sacrifice and the abuse it creates can turn a romantic relationship into a torture chamber. And there is no escape if they have made a commitment to an exclusive and permanent relationship. So when a couple wants to be together for life (cutting off each other's escape routes), they should avoid sacrifice and the suffering it creates.

A Buyer's Rule: The Policy of Joint Agreement

I've found that those who don't feel trapped by their exclusive and permanent commitment usually follow a rule that reminds them to avoid hurting each other. It's what makes them Buyers, instead of Renters. I call this rule the Policy of Joint Agreement: Never do anything without an enthusiastic agreement between you and your partner. Many of these Buyers have never heard of this precise rule, but they know how important it is to make joint decisions because they are committed to each other's happiness for life. And when they hear the rule for the first time, they acknowledge that it's the way they already go about solving their problems.

Later in this book, I will explain the Policy of Joint Agreement to you in more detail and how you can use it to test the value of the Buyer's agreement in your relationship. But for now, I want to simply introduce it to you so that you can see how much sense it makes for Buyers.

When I counsel couples whose marriages are in trouble, at least one spouse is usually a Renter or even a Freeloader. So when I give them this Buyer's rule to teach them how to become thoughtful and sensitive to each other's feelings, they often think it is impractical or even impossible to follow. Yet, if they both follow this rule in spite of how they feel, they begin to experience what Buyers experience—a romantic

---

The Policy of Joint Agreement

Never do anything without an enthusiastic agreement between you and your partner.

---

relationship that is fulfilling for both of them. They avoid doing anything that would hurt one of them, and they learn how to meet each other's emotional needs with enthusiasm. It forces them to negotiate fairly by preventing unilateral decisions. They must discuss each decision before action can be taken.

When a couple makes decisions that lead to an enthusiastic mutual agreement, they create a lifestyle that makes them both happy. So if I can motivate a couple to follow the Policy of Joint Agreement and behave as if they were Buyers, they even-

Consider each other's happiness as equally important. What benefits you both strengthens your relationship. What hurts one of you weakens your relationship.

tually develop the kind of romantic relationship that Buyers develop. And when Renters and Freeloaders see how much better their marriage becomes and how much happier they are, I'm usually able to convert them into permanent Buyers.

The Policy of Joint Agreement encourages couples to consider each other's happiness as equally important. What benefits both of them strengthens their relationship. What hurts one of them weakens their relationship. It just makes good sense to make decisions that are mutually helpful. Why should one person's interests be so important that the interests of the other are ignored? It's a formula for disaster, yet some of the most well-intentioned, intelligent couples do it. That's because their Renter's agreement is in force, and mutual agreement makes very little sense to them.

A romantic relationship agreement, whether it's a Buyer's, Renter's, or Freeloader's agreement, determines the rules that are followed when a conflict arises. The Freeloader refuses to do much at all to resolve the conflict. The Renter is willing to make tentative changes to resolve conflicts, usually short-term efforts that involve personal sacrifice. But only the Buyer views conflicts with a long-term perspective. Unless a resolution is permanent and can be sustained indefinitely, it's not a Buyer's resolution. And that's why the Policy of Joint Agreement is valuable to Buyers. Only decisions that have mutual advantage can create long-term resolutions to conflicts.

Do Buyers Care Unconditionally?

Because Buyers commit to exclusive and permanent care for each other, it may appear that they care unconditionally. But the Policy of Joint Agreement makes care very conditional. It's conditional on the enthusiastic agreement of both partners.

The Freeloader is the only one who believes in unconditional care because he or she expects to be *cared for* uncondi-

The Buyer knows that a relationship must work for both partners or it won't work at all.

tionally. When the subject of care comes up, Freeloaders want a relationship where they are accepted as they are, without any need for change, and without any real expectation for *mutual* care. When a conflict arises, they appeal to their need for unconditional care as an excuse for failing to adjust to the needs of their partner.

The Buyer, on the other hand, is committed to a romantic relationship that will last a lifetime and knows that such a relationship must work for both partners or it won't work at all. When a conflict arises, the Buyer must provide care for both partners simultaneously. It's not a blank check to do whatever the other partner wants or even needs. Instead, it's a form of care that is given in a mutually enjoyable way.

The Policy of Joint Agreement is a rule to create bilateral agreements. Both partners must consider the other's interests and feelings before an enthusiastic agreement can be arranged. The care of a Buyer has conditions that focus attention on what's good for the relationship, rather than what's good for only one partner.

Yet Buyers often think they are caring unconditionally. In fact, at their wedding ceremony, Buyers will often pledge their unconditional care for each other. That's because they want to make each other their highest priority. But that doesn't mean that either of them intends to leave his or her own interests in the dust. When they pledge their unconditional care for each other, it is assumed that both partners' interests will be considered when decisions are made. And that's not really unconditional care.

If, at the wedding ceremony, only one were to pledge unconditional care, and the other were to agree to receive that care but pledge none in return, we would be witnessing pure unconditional care. But that never happens, unless someone forgets his or her lines.

In our wedding ceremony, Joyce and I both memorized our vows. I started first by promising to love Joyce "in joy and in sorrow, in sickness and in health, in plenty and in want, as long as we both shall live." But when it came Joyce's turn, she promised to love me "in joy and in health and in plenty and in wealth, as long as we both shall live." Thankfully for me, time proved that she was a Buyer who was merely nervous at her wedding. Many, however, speak the vows as I spoke them but really mean what Joyce said. They are Freeloaders who are expecting to be cared for unconditionally.

I attended a wedding recently where the minister told the couple to love each other unconditionally, which meant to care for each other without expecting to receive any care. In fact he said they should expect God to meet their needs instead of each other. I almost stood up in the middle of his homily to object! One or both of them could easily assume that they were completely off the hook—a Freeloader's paradise.

Your romantic relationship depends on mutual care for its survival. And if you are unwilling to provide each other

> *Your romantic relationship depends*
> *on mutual care for its survival.*

that mutual care, you may as well pack it in right now. The Freeloader's agreement is a formula for a very short-term relationship—problems are simply never addressed. And the Renter's agreement ultimately leads to a very unsatisfactory way to solve problems—demands, disrespect, and anger prevail. Both of these agreements lead to mounting problems that make romantic relationships seem hopelessly short-lived.

So the goal for every romantic relationship should be to eventually adopt a Buyer's agreement. However, while you will find me praising the virtues of the Buyer's agreement in this book, it's not an agreement designed for those in a dating relationship. When you date, you have not yet committed yourselves to an exclusive and permanent romantic relationship. Even if you are engaged to be married, that commitment has not yet been made. It's only when you marry that you have the opportunity to make the promise to each other, "before God and witnesses," that your care for each other will be exclusive and permanent.

Joyce and I were Renters the moment before we said our wedding vows. Then, a moment later, we were Buyers. If we had dated much longer before marriage, I'm afraid our Renter's agreements would have finished us off. We would have experienced what other couples experience when they've dated too long. They begin to abuse each other with demands and disrespect. Or they become Freeloaders and completely neglect each other. By getting married, Joyce and I were able to set a new course for the creation of a permanent romantic relationship.

Within weeks after our marriage, Joyce told me something I had never known. She did not like playing tennis with me. Remember what I said earlier about recreational companionship and sacrifice? Well, unknown to me, she felt she was sacrificing whenever we played tennis together. Until then, she had been my favorite tennis partner, but she was doing it only to make me happy. She didn't enjoy it. So once we were married, she just stopped playing tennis with me. And there were a host of other changes that she wanted, sacrifices that she had been making for me as a Renter. If I had not been a Buyer at the time of our wedding, I would have felt cheated. "*Now* you tell me," I would have complained.

But I was as willing to form a win-win relationship with Joyce as she was with me. We simply found other recreational activities that we enjoyed as much as I enjoyed tennis. And we were able to make other changes in our relationship that had bothered Joyce. That's the way Buyers approach every conflict. They search for solutions that make them both happy.

If I hadn't agreed to make those changes, Joyce would have been increasingly resentful of everything she did for me. But our marriage and the Buyer's agreement saved our relationship.

Only those relationships that are guided by the Buyer's agreement have any hope for long-term survival because that's the only agreement with long-term objectives. By viewing the romantic relationship as exclusive and permanent, the logical way to solve problems is to make the solutions mutually advantageous. Any other approach to problem solving simply won't keep the romantic relationship alive.

PART 2

The Struggle to Stay Together— What Makes It So Hard?

5

Not on the Same Page

*What Happens
When Agreements Don't Match*

So far we've been assuming that both partners in a romantic relationship are guided by the same agreement. And we've discussed what happens under each. We've noted that relationships between Freeloaders tend to die quickly because the two people avoid conflict, resist change, and often aren't willing to commit care to each other. Renters, on the other hand, are okay for a while, because they do whatever they can to make each other happy. But then they run into problems when their short-sighted, self-sacrificing approach to problem solving breeds resentment and abuse. And we've observed that relationships between Buyers have staying power that is rooted in their commitment to permanent and exclusive care—the kind of care that keeps both partners' best interests in mind.

That's what happens when people are in a romantic relationship with a like-minded individual. But as you probably know, these agreements are not formally hashed out in a romantic relationship, and it's common for two partners to be operating with different agreements.

So what happens when a Freeloader and a Renter are in a romantic relationship? Does that sort of thing ever work out?

What happens to a Freeloader and a Buyer? They both agree that neither should sacrifice, but will that get them very far?

Or how about a Renter and a Buyer? Are they any better off?

Freeloader and Renter: A Common Place to Start

Brenda's letter to Frank in chapter 2 described a Freeloader's typical attitude toward a new romantic relationship. She apparently got the idea from her new love interest, Frank, that he was expecting something from her. And she let him know immediately that there was to be no pressure in this relationship. If she did not give him what he wanted, he should find someone else.

Frank sent me a copy of a letter he wrote in response to Brenda's letter. It was the letter of a Renter in a new relationship. He told her that he loved her and wished only the best for her. He would expect nothing more than the opportunity to meet her needs. He even expressed his unconditional acceptance of her and a willingness to do whatever it was she wanted. That's what Renters usually do in the beginning of a romantic relationship—sacrifice their own interests to make their partner happy. And that's precisely what Brenda expects in a romantic relationship—unconditional acceptance and care.

How long can this relationship last? Will Brenda continue to do whatever she feels like doing while Frank is at her beck and call? As long as Frank is happy in his relationship with

Brenda, that will probably be the case. He will continue to shower her with affection even if she doesn't reciprocate. But sooner or later this one-sided relationship will make him unhappy, and that will inspire him to demand that she start making some sacrifices, just to even things out. When that happens, Brenda will not be pleased.

Instead of letters of unconditional acceptance, Brenda will eventually receive a letter of recrimination. Frank will begin

Sooner or later, this one-sided relationship will make Frank unhappy.

by letting her know that she has failed in meeting her responsibilities in this relationship. But Brenda will reject that notion. After all, she's a Freeloader who believes that neither partner should owe the other anything. She doesn't believe she has any responsibilities in the relationship.

One letter from Frank, and that's all she wrote, so to speak. He may change his mind, try to take it all back, and beg forgiveness for his insensitivity, but by then it will be too late. Brenda will not understand that it was Frank's effort to strike a balance that prompted the letter. Instead, she will think that he was just trying to set her up with his earlier words of unconditional care. And now that she is on to him, it's over.

But even if Brenda gives Frank another chance, I doubt if he could be quite as self-sacrificing again. Brenda has already demonstrated her unwillingness to accommodate his feelings, so Frank has good reason to question her relationship agreement with him. Since he knows that another letter of recrimination won't work, Frank may try being a Freeloader himself. He won't expect anything of Brenda, but he will also be unwilling to go out of his way to meet her needs.

They could try to remain "friends" as Freeloaders indefinitely, but the romantic part of the relationship won't survive. Freeloaders don't remain Lovers very long. Instead, each finds another romantic relationship. They may keep in touch occasionally to keep up the friendship.

Another possibility, of course, is for Brenda to do what I did in my relationship with Joyce—become a Renter. After witnessing Frank's ability to meet her important emotional needs, she may decide that trying to meet his needs would not

Freeloaders don't remain Lovers very long.

be such a bad idea after all, especially if the alternative is to lose Frank. If he did what Joyce did to me—end the relationship—Brenda might have a change of heart.

I suppose I would have been a permanent Freeloader if Joyce had allowed me to get away with it. I had to realize that unless I made an effort to meet Joyce's needs, I'd lose her. That forced me to become a Renter. The adult Freeloaders of this world are sometimes those who have not had sensible partners like Joyce. Instead, they have been spoiled. It's the lazy person's approach to romantic relationships, and sometimes it works well enough to keep some poor partner around for a while.

But most adult Freeloaders spend their lives alone, especially as they age. Brenda's approach to dating doesn't work very well for most people. Most of us must begin a romantic relationship with a demonstration of our ability to meet important emotional needs before the other person will take the relationship seriously. So if you find yourself on a date with a Freeloader like Brenda, it might not hurt to first let that person know what you have to offer. But eventually, breaking off the relationship may be the only way to convert the person into a Renter, or even a Buyer. That's how Joyce converted me.

Freeloader and Buyer: A Romantic Relationship Gone Sour

Freeloaders and Buyers rarely get together in new relationships. But if they do, the Buyer is likely to get seriously burned. Although neither of them believes in sacrifice, only the Buyer is exclusively and permanently committed. So the Freeloader is very likely to cheat on the Buyer early in the relationship. In fact he or she may openly be in other romantic relationships.

Rock stars, sports personalities, and other entertainers who are Freeloaders commonly attract Buyers. These are groupies who have made a one-sided lifelong commitment. Once in a

Buyers and Freeloaders rarely get together in new relationships.

while the entertainer eventually becomes a Buyer (after extensive counseling), fulfilling the dream of the groupie. But it's a very risky proposition. The Buyer is usually left with a broken heart and souvenirs.

Most Freeloader-Buyer combinations are remnants of a relationship that had once been a Buyer-Buyer relationship. If a Buyer becomes a Freeloader, it's usually because he or she has had an affair. Even though a Buyer is committed to an exclusive and permanent relationship, that doesn't necessarily mean he or she can't fall in love with someone else. An innocent friendship can lead to an extraordinary attraction that seems to come out of nowhere, and soon what was totally unexpected becomes irresistible.

Some people can resist such feelings of misdirected love and abandon the new relationship, but the vast majority opt instead to change the agreement in their existing relationship. By becoming a Freeloader instead of a Buyer, they are able to keep an affair alive while still offering hope to the betrayed partner. They can't seem to make up their mind as to which relationship they want the most. They vacillate between the two, and their new beliefs bewilder the betrayed partner.

The betrayed partner tries to argue from the Buyer's perspective: "How could you even think of having another relationship? We are together for life!" The confused unfaithful partner shakes his or her head and finally says, "I guess we were not meant to be together for life."

"*Meant* to be together? We *chose* to be together for life!" points out the betrayed partner. "Have you changed your commitment to me?" The answer, of course, is yes. If it were to be fully understood, the betrayed partner would see that the affair totally changed the unfaithful partner's agreement.

Back in the '50s, psychologist Leon Festinger[1] discovered that it's easier for most people to change their beliefs and values than it is to change their behavior. So when beliefs

---

It's easier for most people to change their beliefs and values than it is to change their behavior.

---

and values are in conflict with behavior, the behavior stays and the beliefs and values usually change. In other words, when someone finds himself or herself having an affair, his or her Buyer's agreement is more likely to be scrapped than is the affair.

In my experience of helping couples restore their marriage after an affair, I've seen that the Buyer's agreement can be restored when the affair has finally ended. And since most affairs end within months after they begin, I usually encourage a betrayed spouse to let the affair "die a natural death" before filing for divorce. I call that Plan A—the betrayed Buyer does his or her best to treat the unfaithful Freeloader with care, even while the affair is still going on. Just as the affair turns the Buyer into a Freeloader, the end of the affair often turns the Freeloader back into a Buyer again.

However, this procedure doesn't usually work if the unfaithful partner never was a Buyer. And even if he or she was a Buyer, it still doesn't always work. So after a reasonable period of time has passed under Plan A, I encourage a betrayed partner to switch to Plan B—the betrayed partner has absolutely no contact with the unfaithful partner until the affair has ended and he or she is committed to becoming a Buyer. Plan B is actually a Renter's plan. It's what Joyce did while I was a Freeloader—she left me.

One advantage to Plan B is that it lessens the suffering that a betrayed partner experiences. Plan A is very painful because it requires caring for someone who is engaged in an

The relationship between Buyer and

Freeloader is a disaster for the Buyer.

act of unbearable thoughtlessness. Some cannot continue that plan for more than a few days because of the stress it causes. So Plan B gives a betrayed partner relief from daily contact with someone who has devastated him or her. And it's also an important step toward ending the relationship if the affair does not end or if the unfaithful partner does not agree to becoming a Buyer.

When I was a Freeloader, Joyce was able to end her relationship with me because she was a Renter. If she had been a Buyer, she could not have done it, because she would have been exclusively and permanently committed to me. So when a Buyer and Freeloader are in a romantic relationship, the most sensible solution, which is to end the relationship with the Freeloader, is not an alternative. That leaves only two other reasonable options. One is to convert the Freeloader back into a Buyer, restoring their mutual care. The other is to convert the Buyer into a Renter or Freeloader, which then allows him or her to leave the relationship.

The relationship between a Buyer and Freeloader is a disaster for the Buyer. While infidelity is usually the most obvious problem, simple neglect can also make the relationship impossible for the Buyer. Freeloaders live their lives as if the Buyer doesn't even exist. Sometimes they leave the Buyer for weeks at a time and return without so much as a "hello." No one can survive a thoughtless relationship for very long.

A Buyer can be an example to the Freeloader of how romantic partners should treat each other. Plan A and Plan B are my recommended strategies for Buyers who have Freeloaders as partners. But in the end, if a Freeloader is not converted, the Buyer should terminate the relationship to avoid a painful life of neglect.

Renter and Buyer: You're Talking but I Don't Hear What You're Saying

Whenever a man and woman in a romantic relationship are operating from different agreements, conversations about conflict are usually bewildering. Beliefs are different, of course, but those conflicting beliefs are not usually stated clearly. As they try to solve problems, they seem to be talking through each other. There is no connection.

Some write it off as the differences between men and women. And it's certainly true that negotiations in romantic relationships can be much more volatile than in any other kind of relationship. But the problem that Renters and Buyers have is that while their perspectives on the relationship are very different, they think they are headed in the same direction. It's only when these differences are clearly brought to their attention that they understand why they don't seem to be able to communicate with each other.

Renters Believe	Buyers Believe
Our relationship is temporary. You may be right for me today and wrong for me tomorrow.	We are together for life.

Renters Believe	Buyers Believe
Our relationship should be fair. What I get should balance what I give.	We both will contribute whatever it takes to make our relationship successful.
As needs change, the relationship may end if needs are difficult to meet.	As needs change, we will make adjustments to meet new needs.
Criticism may prompt me to change if it's worthwhile for me to do so.	Criticism indicates a need for change.
Sacrifice is reasonable as long as it's fair.	Sacrifice is dangerous and to be avoided.
Short-term fixes are fine.	Long-term solutions are necessary.

Now, given these different perspectives, imagine how Sheryl, a Renter, and Brad, a Buyer, will go about solving a problem.

Sheryl and Brad are married with two small children. They both have full-time careers, and when they come home from work, they are both exhausted. It's all they can do to feed their children and get them ready for bed. Their busy schedules have left little time for them to have a romantic relationship, and Sheryl is more aware of the problem than Brad.

"Honey," Sheryl says one evening, "I don't think our relationship is as good as it should be. You don't seem to care about me like you used to."

Brad looks away from the television. "I'm sorry. What would you like me to do?"

"I've just been very unhappy lately," Sheryl explains, almost in tears. "You used to call me at work several times a day, you'd tell me when you were coming home, you'd ask me about how my day went, you'd help me with the kids and the dishes, and after the kids went to bed, you'd watch television with me. Now you ignore me most of the time. I don't know what's happening to us."

Sheryl had been giving this problem quite a bit of thought. She was unhappy and had a good idea of what was missing.

"I'm really sorry I've been neglecting you lately," Brad says. "But you know how crazy it's been at work lately."

"Well, what's more important to you, your work or me?" Sheryl was angry at Brad's excuse.

Brad was not happy with her reaction, but he resisted the temptation to tell her that he was too tired to get into an

Buyers want to find solutions that

work for both partners.

argument. Instead, he offered a suggestion. "Why don't we go to San Francisco next weekend and get reacquainted? I'll make the travel plans if you ask your parents to take care of the children."

"That's just like a man, isn't it?" Sheryl sputtered. "I want a little more attention from you during the week, and all you offer is a weekend of sex. Do you always have to think about what you want? Besides, I've already made plans to go shopping with Kate next weekend. All I want is a little of your precious attention. Do you think you can manage it?"

As a Buyer, Brad wants to find a solution that works well for both of them. He views Sheryl as his exclusive and permanent romantic relationship and is taking her problem seriously. But

Renters want their partners to sacrifice
for them as proof of their care.

his suggestions will always include his own interests as well as hers. That's why a weekend in San Francisco seemed to him something they would both enjoy.

But Sheryl, as a Renter, isn't interested in solutions that would make Brad happy. In fact she wants him to sacrifice for her to prove that he still really cares. So after her initial outburst, she offers a suggestion that requires sacrifice. That will help make up for all the neglect she's been experiencing lately.

"Brad, I'm sorry I got upset with you," she says as she puts her arm around him. "Why don't I call Kate and cancel our shopping date so you can go shopping with me instead? That would make me feel much better."

Now shopping is one of Brad's least favorite things to do, and Sheryl knows it. So now he is in a quandary. Does he sacrifice his own happiness to make Sheryl feel better, or does he continue to negotiate with her to find a mutually enjoyable solution?

"Let's think of some other possibilities," is all Brad can think of to say.

And it's enough to cause Sheryl to blow her cork. She screams, "Fine, now I know why you ignore me so much of the time. You just don't care about me anymore. I'm going to bed."

Sheryl wants Brad to prove he cares about her by making a sacrifice. So any solution he offers that makes him happy fails the test. Brad, on the other hand, is willing to change his behavior, but only in ways that make him comfortable. So any solution she offers that requires his sacrifice will not work for him.

On his own, without actually coming to an agreement with Sheryl, Brad decides to change some of his behavior in ways that give her more attention, yet are comfortable for him to do. He makes a point of calling her during the day and lets her know when he will be coming home in the evening. He also makes more of an effort to help her with the dinner and children.

Sheryl's inappropriate outburst is rewarded by Brad's considerate response. And she overlooks completely the fact that he made an effort to find a mutually agreeable solution to her problem.

If Brad had also been a Renter, he would have entered into a shouting match with Sheryl, calling her all kinds of names,

Buyers and Renters don't do a very good job of negotiating with each other in a relationship.

such as spoiled, selfish, and immature—an accurate, yet disrespectful, description of the way she was behaving. Instead of offering her more care after the argument, he would have withheld care until she apologized, and she would have done the same. After sleeping in separate bedrooms for a week, they would have made up and then would have gone back to sacrificing their own interests to try to make each other happy—an unsustainable solution to their problem. That in turn would have created increasing resentment that would have set them up for their next fight.

If there is one Buyer in a relationship, his or her mature outlook can sometimes overcome the immature approach of the Renter. And the good example set by a Buyer can occasionally convert the Renter to the Buyer's perspective.

But, as my example demonstrates, when a Buyer and Renter are in a romantic relationship, they don't do a very good job negotiating with each other. That's because they have very different ideas about how problems are to be solved.

Two Buyers, on the other hand, take on conflict with safety and comfort. They work out solutions to their problems in ways that can be sustained indefinitely, with both satisfied with the results. Over time they build a life together that is so enjoyable that neither would ever want anything else. They know how to keep their relationship romantic for life.

That's why you and your partner must both be Buyers if you want a romantic relationship that lasts for the long haul.

6

We All Have Split Personalities

Givers and Takers

I've classified romantic relationship agreements into only three basic categories—Buyers, Renters, and Freeloaders. But there are two other categories that may have also occurred to you. They are the Givers and the Takers. Givers are willing to provide care unconditionally—they give until it hurts and then some, expecting nothing in return. And then there are Takers—willing only to take, never to give.

Givers and Takers do exist, but they don't fall into the same type of category as Buyers, Renters, and Freeloaders do. The distinction is fairly complicated, so bear with me as I try to explain Givers and Takers.

I've Given Enough!

Many people come into my office complaining about having been a Giver for years before finally coming to the realization that they're in a relationship with a Taker. These people decide that it's about time for their partner to give a little, and for them to take what they deserve. Then, when their partner comes into my office, I hear the same story. They've done too much giving in the past—now it's time to do some taking. So who's really the Giver and who's really the Taker?

As it turns out, these people are both Givers and Takers. But they are only aware of their own Giver and their partner's Taker. They are ignorant of the fact that they too have a Taker and that their partner has a Giver. The truth is we all have both a Giver and a Taker lurking within us.

The Giver is the part of each of us that is kind and considerate. It follows this rule: *Do whatever you can to make others happy and avoid anything that makes others unhappy, even if it makes you unhappy.* It wants us to make a difference in the lives of others and grows out of our instinct to provide care. It whispers these words of advice to us: *Love unconditionally. Don't think of what others can do for you; think only of what you can do for others. It is more blessed to give than to receive. Give until it hurts.* It wants you to make others happy, even if it is not in your best interest to do so.

Everyone has a Giver. Even the cruelest terrorist does. He is fighting for a cause he thinks will ease the suffering of those he cares for. Some of the most evil, sociopathic people I've ever known have also had a compassionate, loving side.

The Giver's Rule

Do whatever you can to make others happy and avoid anything that makes others unhappy, even if it makes you unhappy.

The Taker's Rule

Do whatever you can to make yourself happy and avoid anything that makes you unhappy, even if it makes others unhappy.

That's why some murderers, rapists, and child molesters can appear to be rehabilitated. They sincerely want—at least some of the time—to avoid ever hurting anyone again.

But the Giver is only half of the story. The other half is the Taker, which is the part of us that is selfish and overbearing. Just as our Giver tries to make others happy or tries to prevent the suffering of others, our Taker tries to make *us* happy and tries to prevent *our* suffering. It's the part of each of us that follows this rule: *Do whatever you can to make yourself happy and avoid anything that makes you unhappy, even if it makes others unhappy.* It wants us to get the most out of life, and it grows out of our basic instinct for self-preservation. It whispers these words of advice to us: *Love yourself unconditionally. Don't be used by others; use them instead. Be sure there's always something in it for you. Get what you need in life, whether or not others want you to have it.* Your Taker wants you to make yourself happy, even if it is not in the best interest of others.

I've found that even those who appear to be the most self-sacrificing have a Taker in the background. If you've ever worked with those who have dedicated their life to the welfare of others—social workers, disaster-relief volunteers, missionaries, and, yes, even psychologists—you know that they are not totally selfless. They have a Taker too.

It's tempting to consider the Giver as our caring nature and the Taker as our thoughtless nature. But that's not what they are. Actually, they are both caring—your Giver cares for others and your Taker cares for you.

Both Giver and Taker also have their thoughtless sides. Your Giver does not care how you feel, and your Taker does not care how others feel. In fact your Giver is willing to see you suffer, even to the point of deep depression, as long as you continue to care about others. Your Taker, on the other hand, is willing to see others suffer if it means that you are happy or are prevented from suffering.

So your Giver and Taker are both good and bad. They are good because both care—the Giver for others and the Taker for you. But they are both bad because they are both thoughtless—the Giver caring nothing for your feelings and the Taker caring nothing for the feelings of others. Because each of them ignores someone's feelings, they are both shortsighted. They fail to understand that you and others should be cared for and protected simultaneously, so that *no one* suffers.

You might think that the Giver and Taker sound a bit like the Buyer and Freeloader, but they are really not at all like either of them. The Giver and Taker are instinctive influences in every one of us that offer very conflicting advice in romantic

---

Your Giver and Taker are both good and bad.

---

relationships. Regardless of the agreement you follow in your romantic relationship, the Giver and Taker will be there to confuse you. The Buyer and Freeloader, on the other hand, are people who have adopted a certain set of beliefs and rules that provide consistent guidance in their romantic relationships. When a problem arises, they turn to the agreement to provide a way to handle the problem. But when an agreement is changed, say from Freeloader to Buyer, a new set of rules are brought to bear on issues in a romantic relationship. We're all selfish and selfless from time to time, depending on whether our Giver or our Taker is dominating our thinking. But the

Buyer's, Renter's, and Freeloader's agreements determine how the Giver and Taker will influence each of us. I'll begin by explaining how the Buyer's and Freeloader's agreements control the Giver and Taker. And then I'll turn to the Renter's agreement.

The Buyer's and Freeloader's Agreements Resist Sacrifice

Both the Buyer's and Freeloader's agreements hold our Giver and Taker in check. Instead of letting us become self-sacrificing or letting us expect self-sacrificing behavior in a romantic rela-

We're all selfish and selfless from time to time, depending on whether our Giver or our Taker is dominating our thinking.

tionship, these two agreements force us to avoid these destructive tendencies. But they do this for very different reasons.

The Freeloader's agreement is based on the assumption that the right relationships should be effortless, so partners should expect of each other only what comes naturally. Freeloaders do not expect sacrifice of each other, but they don't try to adjust to conflicts either. For that reason, the romance in their relationships doesn't last long because they don't go to any effort to accommodate each other's emotional needs.

The Buyer's agreement doesn't allow sacrifice either, because it is based on the assumption that long-term romantic relationships require mutually enjoyable accommodation. But unlike the Freeloader's agreement, it encourages behavioral change to resolve conflicts. It takes the best from the Giver and the Taker, the willingness to care and expect care, and rejects the worst, the willingness to sacrifice and expect sacrifice. As long as the Buyer's agreement is in force, a relationship grows to mutual fulfillment.

The Renter's Agreement Inspires Arguments and Fights

While both the Buyer's and the Freeloader's agreements limit the influence of the Giver and Taker, the Renter's agreement places no restrictions on them. In fact it actually encourages the worst influences of each. It accepts the Giver's willingness to see us sacrifice for others and the Taker's willingness to see others sacrifice for us. And when a couple opens the door to expecting sacrifice of each other, arguments and fights are the result.

Let me explain to you how that works. Renters do not begin their relationship with fights—they usually begin with mutual sacrifice. They rarely deny each other's requests and they do whatever it takes to make each other happy, even if it makes themselves unhappy.

When Jan and Eric first met, they were both very attracted to each other. They were what I have called Lovers, because there was definitely a chemistry between them. Jan soon learned that Eric enjoyed watching sporting events on television, so she willingly watched them with him, even though she would have preferred watching movies instead. Eric learned that Jan enjoyed talking—for hours at a time. So when they couldn't get together for a date, he stayed on the telephone talking to her long after he really enjoyed the conversation. During the first few weeks of their relationship, they did whatever it took to make each other happy. They were in the first phase of a Renter's romantic relationship in which both of their Givers were in full control.

As long as both partners are happy, Givers stay in control. But sacrifice eventually takes its toll. Since the care they provide each other is somewhat unpleasant, it never becomes a habit for either of them. Instead, each time they meet each other's needs, they must do it deliberately instead of effortlessly, the way habits are usually performed. That means that their care is inconsistent, taking place only when they are in a good mood and willing to sacrifice for each other.

Jan didn't watch sporting events on television with Eric because she enjoyed them; she did it because it made him

Sacrifice eventually takes its toll.

happy. And Eric didn't talk to Jan for hours because he enjoyed talking to her that long; he did it just to make her happy. In fact much of what they did for each other was enjoyable for one of them but somewhat unpleasant for the other. As a result, very little of their care for each other developed into habits that were consistent and effortless.

A relationship based on sacrifice does *not* keep partners in a good mood. In fact over time it tends to create a very *bad* mood between partners. And whenever we are in a bad mood, our Takers come to our rescue. *Are you unhappy? That's because you've been giving too much. Now it's time for you to do some taking*, our Taker whispers to us.

Requests that were rarely denied in the beginning of a Renter's relationship start being denied as soon as the effects of their sacrifice sink in. When that happens, the second phase of a Renter's romantic relationship begins—requests that are now denied are turned into demands. *If you won't give me what I need when I ask you for it, I'll make you to give it to me!*

One day Jan decided she didn't want to watch another sporting event on television with Eric. Her Taker was slowly but surely gaining strength and her Giver was weakening. She

A relationship based on sacrifice does

not keep partners in a good mood.

took the remote control and announced that on this day she would decide what they would watch.

But this wasn't just any day. This was the day that Eric's favorite football team, the Pittsburgh Steelers, was finally in the playoffs against the defending champion Baltimore Ravens. He had to watch this game whether Jan liked it or not.

"Don't kid around with me. Give me the remote control," Eric demanded.

Demands are usually the first step in an argument. When one partner tells the other what to do, it's because his or her Taker suggests that the demand is reasonable. *After all*, explains the Taker, *your partner owes you what you are demanding. You deserve it. And your partner should provide it, even if it requires sacrifice.*

Eric had spent two hours talking to Jan on the telephone the night before the big game—because that's what she wanted to do. So he decided that now was his turn to do what he wanted to do, and that was to watch the Steelers beat the Ravens.

Jan's Taker didn't quite see it that way, however. She wasn't in the mood to give Eric what he demanded. Besides, his demand was totally rude. What right did he have to tell her what to do? Jan's Taker advised noncompliance. *Whatever he demands, don't do it.*

"Eric, whenever I've come over to watch television, we've always watched what you wanted to see. Don't you think I should be able to watch something I like once in a while?" Jan's Taker put the words right into her mouth.

If Jan's and Eric's Givers had been included in this discussion, the demand would have been softened or eliminated

In a relationship between Renters, when a Taker steps forward, it pushes the Giver aside.

entirely, because the Giver never wants us to do anything that would make someone unhappy. And if a demand by Eric somehow slipped out, Jan's Giver would have encouraged her to comply just this once. But in a romantic relationship between Renters, when a Taker steps forward, it pushes the Giver aside. And when demands are made, Givers are usually nowhere to be found. Instead, the partner being told what to do is encouraged by his or her Taker to fight fire with fire.

Eric was not persuaded by Jan's appeal to fairness. Maybe she could watch what she wanted next time, but this time it would be the Steelers and Ravens.

"Look, if you want to watch some stupid movie, watch it some other time," Eric responded. "Today we'll be watching history in the making."

"History for fools, maybe. Or for fat, lazy men who would rather watch others get some exercise instead of getting it themselves." With that comment, Jan threw the remote control at Eric.

Most fights begin with demands, but it doesn't take long for the demands to turn into disrespectful comments of some kind. That in turn usually leads to an angry outburst, and the fight is on. Jan and Eric had planned to spend a romantic Sunday afternoon together, but their argument got in the way. As soon as Eric got the remote control, he switched on the football game, and the fight was over.

Sadly, fights often lead to the fulfillment of the demand. That's why they exist in romantic relationships. They actually work enough of the time to make them useful, albeit at the expense of the relationship. After their fight, Jan was in no mood for romance, and she left before halftime.

If you and your partner are Renters, you've probably had lots of arguments. And if you tend to argue with your partner,

If you and your partner tend to argue, you must be Renters.

you must be a Renter. That's because Freeloaders don't even try to accommodate each other, and Buyers would rather negotiate than argue. I'm not saying that Freeloaders and Buyers *never* argue. But because of their beliefs about relationships, neither feels that an argument is ever appropriate, and that makes their arguments very rare.

Freeloaders don't want to argue, because they feel that they should never force their partner to do anything. They should do for each other only what comes naturally. And Buyers don't want to argue because that won't help them find solutions

Restrictions must be placed on your Giver and Taker.

that have their mutual enthusiastic agreement. Since both Freeloaders and Buyers do not tolerate sacrifice in a romantic relationship, arguments make no sense to them.

To avoid the disastrous consequences of arguments that can lead to garden-variety fights or even domestic abuse, restrictions must be placed on your Giver and Taker. And that's precisely what Buyers do. Since they follow the Policy of

Joint Agreement, which requires mutual enthusiastic agreement, they must learn to care for each other in ways that do not require sacrifice for either of them. Fights make no sense under those conditions, so Buyers don't fight. No demands, no disrespect, no angry outbursts, just a willingness to provide whatever care is needed in a way that is enjoyable for both.

7

No Such Thing as a Free Lunch

Dependency and Control

Sally was raised in a very traditional home. Her mother cared for the children while her father supported the family. But her mother paid a big price for being a homemaker—her husband controlled her. His word was law, and she was forced to do whatever he felt was right. Long after Sally and her two sisters left home, her father continued to control his wife, and Sally vowed she would never put up with such a controlling husband.

When Sally first met Greg at the office where they both worked, she was blown away by his intelligence and good looks. She could hardly carry on a conversation with him because she found him so attractive. And then, when he actually asked her to go on a date, she considered herself the luckiest girl in the world. As they continued to date, Sally read books on men and what they wanted, and she tried to do everything to please Greg. She was absolutely crazy about him and rarely denied him anything. He became the center of her life, so much so that she completely forgot about what *she* needed.

The first sign of trouble came after Greg met some of her friends. He was very quiet on their ride home together. "What's the matter, Greg?" Sally asked.

"What is it that you see in these people?" Greg answered. "I'm surprised that you would want any of them as your

Greg became the center of Sally's life, so much so that she completely forgot about what she needed.

friends. They are all going nowhere, and all they talk about is the fact that they're going nowhere."

"But I've known these people most of my life. We've been friends for years. They were probably intimidated by your success and felt inferior to you. I think all of them are great, but you first have to get to know them."

Getting to know them was not in Greg's plans. In fact he let Sally know that he didn't even want her to spend time with them because they would be a bad influence on her. He wanted her to cut off her contact with them.

The truth was that Greg was jealous of her friends. She obviously liked being with them, and he felt threatened by her attraction to them, especially to Curt, who hung around her the whole evening. But instead of explaining his own insecurity, he showed disrespect for Sally's friends and demanded that she stop seeing them, which is what she did.

In spite of the warning signs, Sally married Greg, and after their first child arrived, he decided that she should quit her job to become a full-time stay-at-home mom. She agreed, with reservations, remembering how being a homemaker had trapped her mother and hoping the same wouldn't happen to her.

But it did. As soon as she left her job, Greg became very

critical of her. The house wasn't quite clean enough; she wasn't quite thin enough; they didn't make love quite often enough. Once in a while, he would fly into a rage and lecture her on some mistake he thought she had made.

When their second child arrived, Sally became very depressed. She felt completely dependent and without any control of her life. She felt her identity slipping away. So she began seeing a counselor to help her understand her depression and how to overcome it.

She and her counselor spent a few sessions going over her past, particularly the roles played by each member of her family. They talked about how she had fallen into the same role as her mother and how her husband had gained control over her, the same way her father had control over her mother. The more they talked about it, the more terrified Sally became. Over the course of a few sessions with her counselor, however, she began to understand her depression more clearly. Her marriage had almost killed her spirit, but not quite.

Within a few weeks, Sally had a new perspective on life, one that opened up opportunities that she had not allowed herself to consider. Once that happened, she made immediate plans to break out of Greg's grip. Her counselor suggested that she go back to work to escape Greg's financial control over her. She explained to Sally that control of money was the key to gaining control over the rest of her life.

Until then, Sally had to come to Greg for every penny she spent, and he insisted that she account for every one of them. Her performance as a "good" wife usually determined her allowance. She often felt like a prostitute. But after she found a job, the money she earned was hers to spend on what she needed. She even opened her own checking account and got her own credit cards. She no longer had to cater to Greg's whims or try to meet his unreasonable demands.

Within a few weeks, her depression was completely gone. She was cured. She missed her children while she was at work, but she found good child care for them. Most important, however, her daughters had a mom they would never have to pity. She was breaking a tradition of male dominance, and

Sally didn't want a divorce; all she really wanted was for Greg to stop trying to control her.

she felt that her example would spare them the pain that she and her mother had experienced.

But Greg didn't take Sally's newly found independence sitting down. He did everything he could to try to get her back into his trap. He criticized her care of the children and even told them that her job was more important to her than they were. But the more demanding, disrespectful, and angry he became, the more convinced Sally was that she had made the right decision.

At first, she argued with him, but eventually she gave up trying. She finally asked him for a separation because she was a better person when he was not around. When she was away from him, she could think clearly, have less anxiety, and feel in control of herself. When she was with him, however, she was tense, confused, and felt that she was losing control again. Yet she didn't want a divorce. All she really wanted was for Greg to stop trying to control her.

Marriage Can Be a Trap

One reason couples are reluctant to marry these days is that once married, they know that they risk being trapped and controlled by each other. Sally's mom certainly had that experience, and Sally didn't want it repeated in her own life. But she didn't know how to prevent it from happening.

Sally became trapped because she and Greg unwittingly used the Renter's strategy for solving problems. At the time of their marriage, they may have actually made an exclusive and permanent commitment to each other. But because they failed to use the Buyer's problem-solving strategy, Sally's commitment was a cruel trap.

In the beginning of Renters' relationships, they rarely deny each other's requests. So merely mentioning a need is all it takes to find fulfillment. But after their Givers' sacrifice for

Buyers don't try to control each other.

each other starts to take its toll, requests no longer work. When that happens, Renters try to get what they need from each other the only way their Takers know how to do it—with demands, disrespect, and anger. In other words, they try to control each other.

Sally escaped Greg's control over her the way most Renters escape—with separation or divorce. But before they can escape, they must break the bond of dependence. And that's what Sally's counselor encouraged her to do by finding a job that gave her financial independence.

Another solution would have been for Sally to tough it out, as her mother was doing. She accepted her role as prisoner in her husband's home and was trying to make the most of it. That's a solution that Sally wasn't willing to consider after she saw what it had done to her mother.

But the best solution would have been for Greg and Sally to adopt the Buyer's approach to problem solving. That's because Buyers don't try to control each other. They don't make demands, show disrespect, or lose their temper. They solve their problems by negotiating solutions that are in their mutual interest.

Dependency and control are so destructive that no romantic relationship can survive them. Sally's mother may have endured her dependency and her husband's control, but they completely destroyed her romantic relationship with him. Anyone who wants an exclusive and permanent romantic relationship simply cannot allow dependency or control to exist.

What Are Dependency and Control?

Nobody I know likes to be controlled by someone else. I don't like to be controlled, and my wife, Joyce, doesn't like

Nobody likes to be controlled by someone else.

to be controlled. But as much as I am opposed to anybody controlling anybody else, once in a while Joyce will let me know that she thinks I'm trying to control her. At the time, I don't agree, but she insists that I am. When she says that, what does she mean?

To some extent, the feeling of being controlled once in a while may be inevitable in any romantic relationship. But I believe there are appropriate ways to minimize that feeling when it is not intended. And when it is intended, there are ways to identify the monster for what it is—a potentially fatal mistake that ruins romantic relationships.

Dependency

Let's start by defining the terms. The first word I'd like to discuss with you is *dependency*.

If I were to begin mailing you a check for ten thousand dollars each month, asking for nothing in return, you would undoubtedly be extremely pleased and grateful. You would most certainly like me, and you would regard me as a very generous person. You might put at least some of the money into savings, since you would now have more money than you were used to spending. But if you were like most people, after a few months, the extra income would be absorbed into an improved quality of life. You might also question the wisdom of working fifty hours a week for three thousand dollars a month. So you might decide to quit your job to do something you really enjoy instead. If that happened, you would become dependent on me for that monthly check.

Since my gift was one-sided—I gave you something, but you did nothing for me in return—you would be truly depen-

You are dependent when what you receive is
not balanced by what you give in return.

dent. In other words, you are dependent when what you receive is not balanced by what you give in return. Generosity and a willingness to sacrifice are usually the motives behind such one-sided giving, motives we all value. But when there is no reciprocity, it creates dependency.

It's our Giver's approach to caring for others—it encourages us to give, expecting nothing in return. And when Renters are in the beginning phase of a romantic relationship, their Givers are given the green light to create dependency. Each person tends to give to the other unconditionally and sacrificially. Of course, our Giver doesn't want to create dependency, but that's how things turn out whenever we give unconditionally.

Sally began giving to Greg unconditionally as soon as he started dating her. She rarely denied him anything and even left all her friends just to make him happy. It was Sally's Giver at work, creating expectations in Greg that turned out to be unrealistic. But that's what Givers do. They give without wanting anything in return—and that's unrealistic.

Greg did the very same thing. His Giver also gave to Sally unconditionally. He knew what she liked about him, his attentiveness, his admiration of her, his affection, and his good looks, so he made sure she got the best of what he had to offer. He did things for her that made him irresistible to her.

What's wrong with giving unconditionally? you may ask. *Isn't that the way all romantic relationships should be*? As bizarre as it may sound, this is actually how abusive relationships begin. Because the Giver is allowed to operate without restriction, the Taker is also given free rein. And that's when the trouble begins.

Control

Time to look at the second word—*control*.

After a while, you may start feeling a little nervous about your growing dependence on that monthly check I am sending you. What if I stopped sending it? How would you compensate for the lost income? You would probably begin asking yourself those and other questions about the wisdom of having gotten into such a situation. But in spite of growing apprehension, you are still grateful for the gift as long as it keeps coming.

What if one day I told you that there was something you could do for me to earn that check? *Wait a minute*, you might think. *I thought this was a gift! What is this about "earning" the check*?

As alarmed as you might be, you feebly ask what it is I want. Suppose I want you to mow my lawn once a week, and you have to do it yourself—you can't hire someone to do it. How would you feel about mowing my lawn for twenty-five hundred dollars a week? That's a lot of money to be paid for mowing a lawn. But compared to the original ten thousand dollars a month for doing nothing, you may start to feel controlled by me. When you are out mowing my lawn, you may be wondering what little tasks I will think of next.

You probably would want to do something for me anyway, after receiving my ten-thousand-dollar checks for a

Dependency and control go hand in hand.

few months, but you would want it to be a gift, not an assignment. If you are like most people, you probably feel that I tricked you. You think I gave you the money to make you dependent on me, because once you are dependent, I can try to control you. Before long, I may have you completely enslaved.

You can see where I'm headed with this illustration. Dependency and control go hand in hand. Once you reach a point where you depend on someone, he or she is in a position to control you.

While the Giver sets up dependency by encouraging you to give unconditionally, the Taker has no such generous motives. It looks at the situation and sees it as totally unfair. *Why give ten thousand dollars a month for nothing in return*? the Taker cries out. *You should at least have your lawn mowed*!

The Taker sees the Giver's plan as terribly flawed, but concocts a way of making it fair. It will encourage me to extract ever-increasing work from you to compensate for the ten-thousand-dollar "gift." Technically, since the Taker is not really a good judge of fairness, it will try to extract from you as much as possible, eventually getting far more than the ten thousand dollars might be worth to you. Remember, the Taker takes unconditionally, just as the Giver gives unconditionally.

At what point would you say, "Enough is enough! You can keep your money. I'm going back to my boring three-thousand-dollar-a-month job!" You may have already become accustomed to a ten-thousand-dollar-a-month quality of life. Giving it up to avoid my increasingly burdensome demands may be a tough assignment.

And that's what Greg did with Sally. After she became financially dependent on him, he started making demands that she clean the house better, lose weight, and make love to him more often. These were not requests. They were demands for what he felt she owed him for what he was doing for her.

I imagine that Greg made many contributions to Sally's life, but the one that she saw as most important was his financial support of her. She felt that if she were to get out from under his control, she would have to earn her own financial support. And that's exactly what her counselor suggested she do, and what she eventually did. Once Sally became financially independent, Greg lost financial control and she felt great. His abusive efforts to regain control did nothing but drive her away from him because she was no longer dependent.

Amazingly enough, Sally was willing to be reunited with Greg. Her motive to let him return to her had quite a bit to do with all of the other things that he did for her. But first she wanted him to stop trying to control her. And that would require a new strategy.

Interdependence: The Buyer's Alternative

Here's the third concept I want to discuss with you—*interdependence*. In an interdependent relationship, two people come to depend on each other not through gift giving but through negotiation, keeping each other's interests in mind. This is not the dependency we have just discussed, because after a transaction is completed, no one owes anybody anything. One person meets a need in a way that is enjoyable in exchange for the other person meeting their need in a way that is also enjoyable. The selflessness of the Giver and selfishness of the Taker are overcome by mutual interests, and that eliminates the risk of control.

If Greg had never made demands, shown disrespect, or lost his temper with Sally, the issue of control would not have been raised. But when Sally did not fulfill Greg's requests, he didn't

In an interdependent relationship, two people come to depend on each other not through gift giving but through negotiation, keeping each other's interests in mind.

know what else to do. Without the Renter's strategy, how could he have a clean house, a slim wife, and frequent lovemaking? And when he was first dating Sally, how could he have avoided those friends of Sally's who threatened him so much?

As I mentioned at the beginning of this book, I believe that we cannot adequately meet our own intimate needs in life. Someone whom we love and who loves us must meet them for us. These intimate needs include affection, intimate conversation, sexual fulfillment, recreational companionship, admiration, and many others. When someone meets these needs, we fall in love with that person and want to be with them for the rest of life so that our needs can be continually met. In other words, we come to depend on that person to meet our intimate needs. That's what romantic relationships are all about.

So when one person in a romantic relationship stops meeting the other person's needs, it creates a crisis. After all, the purpose of a romantic relationship is the meeting of these important emotional needs. If important emotional needs are no longer met, it's no longer a romantic relationship.

Renters respond to such a crisis by making demands, showing disrespect, and losing their temper. But if those behaviors are forbidden, what's left? My answer, of course, is the Buyer's strategy—negotiation with mutual feelings and interests in mind.

When two people in a romantic relationship understand each other's emotional needs and have enthusiastically agreed to meet them for each other, not as gifts but as a joint commitment to insure the success of their relationship, they are interdependent. As long as the way they meet these needs take the interests of both into account, and their promises that the needs will be met are kept, no one feels controlled.

But hardly any romantic relationships have that kind of clear understanding. Most of them seem to be more like my ten-thousand-dollar-a-month offer. *I will meet all of your needs and expect nothing in return. T*hat's what love does to our reasoning capacity. It makes us pure Givers, and remember, our Giver thinks only of others, never of ourselves. We all are tempted to do it, even though it creates dependency and the risk of control.

When Sally married Greg, what did she understand the terms to be? Did she agree to meet his emotional needs in return for his meeting hers? I doubt it. She probably didn't even know what her emotional needs were. She married Greg because she loved him and thought he loved her. She didn't give much thought to how she came to feel that way.

So when Greg worked harder to support her so she could be home with their daughters, she simply felt that he was following through on the unconditional love he had promised. Greg, on the other hand, had his own set of expectations that had never been clearly expressed to Sally. He wanted her to keep the house clean, stay thin, and have sex with him as often as he wanted. And he felt his extra work entitled him to extra performance on her part.

After their children arrived, Sally failed to meet his needs in the way he expected them to be met, so his Taker was roused, and sadly, he allowed himself to become influenced. He became a monster, someone no one could tolerate.

Sally did not consider her care of Greg to be part of a deal. She saw it as a gift. Her unconditional gifts to him were housework, attractiveness, and sex. And he had the nerve to criticize her for not giving him more, the ungrateful wretch!

Technically, Sally would have been upset with Greg if he had not found a job. And Greg would have felt just as controlled as Sally if she had demanded that he keep looking for a job until he found one. After all, Greg's income was a gift to Sally, not a responsibility, right?

All of this confusion and sadness could have been avoided if Sally and Greg had started their marriage with a mature understanding of what they meant to each other. They were in this relationship to meet each other's intimate emotional needs, not as gifts but as part of a mutually enthusiastic agreement. If they had adopted the Buyer's approach to implementing that agreement, Sally would never have had a reason to feel controlled or to leave Greg.

Sally felt controlled partly because she was forced to do something she did not want to do—meet Greg's needs the way he wanted them met. If she had come to a negotiated agreement with him, she might have met them in a way that she wanted to meet them, and then they would have both been happy. But she also felt controlled because she could not say no to him without fear of his becoming emotionally distant or argumentative or reducing her allowance. By giving him the sex he wanted, she may have found him to be much easier to live with, with more money in her pocket, but her resentment grew every time they made love.

In an effort to avoid Greg's unpleasant reaction, Sally tried to do whatever she could to make him happy so that he would not threaten her, but nothing she did worked. The harder she

A Buyer's agreement creates an interdependent relationship.

tried, the higher his standards became. In her effort to reach those higher standards she completely lost sight of her own opinions, feelings, and needs, and she found herself losing her identity.

Remembering her mother's experience, and with the help of a counselor, she snapped herself out of her anxiety and depression by overcoming her dependence on Greg's financial support. She got a job so that she could support herself, and her final act of independence was to actually move away into her own apartment.

Sally feels much better now than she did when she was living with Greg. That's because breaking out of her dependent relationship with him was one solution to her problem. Once independent, she no longer felt controlled by him. She regained her identity.

If she were to go back to live with him again, what could he do to prevent a recurrence of his control over her? How could she avoid feeling depression and anxiety all over again? They would need to trade in their Renter's agreement for a Buyer's agreement.

A Buyer's agreement creates an interdependent relationship. A couple negotiates to get what they each need in marriage. Negotiations begin with the assumption that neither of them *owes* anything to the other, but each of them *needs* something from the other. Their goal, then, is to find a way to meet each other's needs in a mutually enjoyable way. No demands, intimidation, or trying to make the other person feel guilty is permitted, because it's through respectful and thoughtful negotiation that an interdependent relationship is created.

If you feel controlled in your romantic relationship, it's because you and your partner don't negotiate with each other. Instead, you either sacrifice (giving whatever the other wants even when it is not in your best interest to do so) or you demand

Buyers begin with the assumption that neither of them owes the other anything but that each of them needs something from the other.

(forcing the other person to give you what you want). Those are the strategies of the Giver and Taker, and those strategies create dependency and control.

I suggest that you and your partner abandon those worthless strategies for resolving conflict. Instead, enter into thoughtful negotiations, where neither of you makes any demands or sacrifices. Make your needs known to each other, and then work together to meet those needs in ways that are comfortable for both of you.

Use the Policy of Joint Agreement to guide you. Avoid compromises that do not meet with your mutually enthusiastic agreement. That way, every decision you make will hold up over time and will help you create a very fulfilling romantic relationship.

Once you and your partner have decided to try to negotiate respectfully, you may need some help in learning how to go about it. In chapters 11 and 12 of this book, I will describe the basic steps I suggest you take whenever you are in conflict with each other. Follow my advice, and you will learn to have a relationship where neither of you controls the other.

8

Buyer Resistant

The Electric Fence Personality

Psychologists are known for their interest in personalities, and I'm no exception. I've even created my own names for some of the personality types I've encountered. But there is something I've noticed for years in regard to Buyers, Renters, and Freeloaders—there is a personality type that has a very difficult time being a Buyer. I call it the Electric Fence personality. I'll explain what I mean by that a little later in this chapter, but first let me give you a brief overview of how personality influences romantic relationships.

Personality and Romance

Personality is a characteristic way of approaching life that makes an individual's choices somewhat predictable. For example, a People-Pleaser personality causes a person to go to a great deal of trouble to make sure that everyone likes him or her. Whenever a choice is made, the question this personality asks is, *What alternative will make people like me the most?* And that's the one he or she chooses.

In choosing a lifetime mate, People-Pleasers will often marry their Likers or even their Dislikers instead of their Lovers. That's because they try so hard to make people like them that even their Dislikers are impressed enough by their willingness to accommodate that they consider them for marriage. But then, after marriage, the effort it takes People-Pleasers to make their Dislikers happy causes so much stress that they often suffer from chronic headaches and sickness.

Another example of a personality is the Perfectionist. This personality tries to make decisions that are perfect in every way possible. It shouldn't surprise you to know that these people are usually very indecisive. They can't make up their minds, because the perfect choice is very elusive. But they sure know a lot about imperfection, and, as a result, they are very hard to please.

Perfectionists tend not to be anyone's Lover for long. That's because they can always find the fly in the ointment. There is always something about the other person that needs to be improved. While People-Pleasers tend to *get* headaches trying to please a critical partner, Perfectionists tend to *give* headaches to their partner, who always seems to come up short of the mark.

People-Pleasers and Perfectionists are just two of the many different personality types that influence our decisions in a

---

Personality

A characteristic way of approaching life that makes an individual's choices somewhat predictable.

---

unique way. If you think about the people you know, I'm sure you can identify a number of others as well. You may even be able to identify your own personality if you try to think of the emotional reasons that tend to guide your decisions.

Many of us are a combination of different personality types. For example, consider someone with both a People-Pleaser and a Perfectionist personality. As you may well imagine, such a person tends to both give and get headaches in a romantic relationship. Each characteristic operates simultaneously, which makes these people want to please their partner yet also makes them difficult to please themselves. Such people

The emotional reasons that tend to guide your decisions may indicate your personality type.

usually end up with Freeloaders because Freeloaders don't care whether or not they please anyone, yet they are relatively easy to please. Since Freeloaders tend to come and go, it's a revolving door experience for those with this dual personality, but at least they are not lonely.

The Giver and Taker that I introduced to you in chapter 6 are sometimes considered dual personalities, but I don't think of them that way. That's because they are a part of each of us—we all have both of them. On the other hand, personality types that psychologists have identified are found in some people but not others.

I've studied dozens of personality types over the years and have discovered how each of them helps or hinders people in romantic relationships. And I've learned how to guide couples with very different personalities into a fulfilling marriage.

But there is one personality that I have always found particularly troublesome. People with this personality seem to have more trouble with romantic relationships in general, and marriage in particular, than those with any other personality. I call it the Electric Fence personality (EFP).

Running into the Electric Fence

The path of life for people with an EFP has an electric fence running along each side of it. Not only that, but their stroll down that path takes place at night, the flashlight they use to find their way is very dim, and the path takes many sharp turns. That makes it difficult for them to see the electric fence at the edge of the path, and they often stumble into it. As long

> *EFPs do whatever they can to back*
> *away from their electric fences.*

as these people are in the middle of the path, they are usually very happy and optimistic about life. But when they touch the fence, they get a rude shock and will do anything to get away from it and back onto the path. Once back on the path, they're happy again.

From the definition of personality, we learn that an individual with a certain personality will have fairly predictable behavior, and this holds true for EFPs. When they touch their electric fence, they do whatever they can to back away from it. They tend to either panic or fly into a rage in an effort to escape, because the experience is so painful to them. And anyone who is with them when they hit the fence knows with certainty that they are very upset when it happens. But because others do not have the same electric fence to contend with, they often view the panic or rage as overreaction. They don't realize that they would react the same way if they had the same electric fence along the sides of their path through life.

Doug wanted to make Valentine's Day very special for Beth, so he took her to one of the most exclusive restaurants in Minneapolis. But as they were seated, Doug could see that Beth was very uncomfortable with the booth they were given.

"See if we can sit at a table," Beth suggested. "I really don't like this booth."

So Doug asked the waiter if they could be moved to a table. But this was Valentine's Day, and all of the tables were already taken. "I'm sorry, but there are no tables available this evening," the waiter replied.

Before Doug had a chance to respond, Beth shouted, "Well, then, *make* a table available!"

Doug was stunned. "Honey, there are no tables. We'll be fine here, waiter. We'll be ready to give you our order in a few minutes."

"Why would you tell him that we'll be fine? I'm not fine here! I already told you. I want a table!" Beth shouted. She was getting increasingly upset.

"Would you please calm down! Everyone's looking at us," Doug whispered.

Beth had hit her electric fence—the booth. For her, it was

Beth had hit her electric fence.

intolerable to sit there, and she wanted to move away from it quickly. She made that very clear to both the waiter and to Doug, but neither accommodated her wishes. So after giving Doug a piece of her mind, she got up and walked out of the restaurant.

Doug went after her, but instead of suggesting that they find another restaurant that evening, he began to blame her for her reaction. "What is wrong with you? The booth was just fine. You know you can't always have *everything* you want in life," Doug pontificated.

That did it. Beth flew into a rage and called Doug every name that came into her head. But she still had the presence of mind to hail a cab, and that's how she got back to the safety and comfort of her apartment.

Beth had actually felt much better as soon as she was outside of the restaurant, but when Doug started blaming her for

---

EFPs don't know where their
electric fences are located.

---

her reaction, he shoved her into another electric fence with his disrespectful comments. And he was even suggesting that she should go back to the electric fence she had just left!

Doug went home very bewildered that night. He called Beth, and she seemed in remarkably good spirits, considering what they had both been through.

"We've had dinner in booths before. Why didn't you like the booths there?" Doug asked.

"I just felt claustrophobic in that booth. I'm sorry I ruined our evening together, but you shouldn't have tried to make me stay there," Beth replied.

There was no real apology for all the nasty things Beth had said to Doug. In fact Beth couldn't really remember what she had said. All she could remember was his suggestion that she was spoiled. After she had a chance to think about it, she figured that he was right. She did want things her way.

Those with an EFP don't know where their fence is located because of the sharp turns in the path and their dim flashlight, so they stumble into it quite regularly, expressing panic or anger whenever it happens. Whoever is close by is likely to be blamed for their unpleasant experience.

Once off the fence, however, they usually return to a very happy state and try to forget the incident. Since the path takes sharp turns, they give up hope of learning from past experience, because the fence will be somewhere else next time. So they figure it's best to just forget the whole thing.

These people have remarkably little insight into what makes them happy and sad. That's why I use the analogy of the dim flashlight and sharp turns in the path. When I have a client with such a personality, it often seems that I understand his or her likes and dislikes better than the client does, because my flashlight seems to be brighter than the EFP's flashlight. I remember what his or her last electric fence looked like, and to me the next one often looks very similar.

EFPs' lack of insight makes them very impulsive and great risk takers because they don't seem to learn from their past

The way to get along with EFPs is to follow them on their life path.

painful experiences. And they are also usually optimistic and cheerful, as long as they are in the middle of their pathway, because they don't like to think about past painful jaunts into their electric fence.

Others may join an EFP on his or her path. They are not affected by the electric fence, so they can wander on and off the path and remain unscathed. They encourage the EFP to follow, but once the electric fence is touched, he or she cannot follow. If pressured to follow, the EFP usually becomes very angry, blaming the other person for causing him or her so much pain.

Obviously the way to get along with people who have this EFP is to *follow* them on *their* life path, because they cannot usually follow you on yours. These people may seem very selfish and uncompromising, but you would behave the same way if you had an electric fence along the sides of your path of life.

Rule Resistant

EFPs have a terrible time with other people's rules, because those rules often lead them into their fences. As children, they have trouble with authority for the same reason. At first, they try to follow rules and obey authority, but the pain of the electric fence is so great that they soon learn to be a rule unto themselves, and they ignore what others tell them to do. Abandoning rules, in turn, usually leads them into all kinds of trouble, and many of these people, especially men, end up in prison.

So when I introduce the Policy of Joint Agreement, the Buyer's rule, to one of these people, it's almost immediately rejected—simply because it's a rule. I must spend a consider-

EFPs have a terrible time with

other people's rules.

able amount of time trying to explain that the rule is in their best interest and will never lead them into their electric fence before I'm able to get to first base. But even then, it's viewed with considerable skepticism. They ignore the fact that *they* must be enthusiastic about a decision before it is made, and all they can think about is the fact that their partner must be enthusiastic about their decisions. They've learned to overlook the feelings of others as the only way to quickly get off their electric fence. So when I tell them that they must take their partner's feelings into account, they don't believe it's possible.

EFPs are most comfortable with the Freeloader's philosophy. They believe that it is immoral to ask anyone to change on their behalf, or for anyone to ask them to change, because they've found change to be so painful. As long as someone walks on their path, they can have a great relationship, but if that person decides to wander off the path, they cannot follow. Their effort to accommodate that person by following him or her leads them right into their electric fence. Panic sets in when

EFPs are most comfortable with the Freeloader's philosophy.

EFPs suspect that a permanent relationship will trap them in a lifetime of electric shocks. The great relationship they had for a while turns into a mess as they find their partner on the other side of the fence much of the time. Eventually that person is not even their friend because he or she has wandered too far away from the path.

As you might expect, EFPs are very likely to have affairs. Since they have such difficulty with adjustments, they are usually in a romantic relationship only with people who happen to be on their path. But when those people leave the path, it's much too painful for EFPs to follow, so they move on to a relationship with someone else who happens to be on their path. They are the ones who originated the saying *If you can't be with the one you love, love the one you're with*.

Understandably, EFPs often view the Buyer's agreement as a trap, because they have had so many experiences of being shocked by the electric fence while trying to accommodate others. They associate an exclusive and permanent commitment with a life of suffering.

But the Buyer's agreement does not lead to suffering, even for an EFP. In fact the Buyer's rule, the Policy of Joint Agreement, specifically disallows suffering by *either* partner. So even EFPs have nothing to fear from a Buyer's agreement. Their only restraint is that they cannot make choices that run roughshod over the feelings of their partner.

If EFPs are to become Buyers, they need to know that there is an approach to romantic relationships that gives them freedom to stay away from their electric fence and keeps their partner on their side of the fence. How? I've found two basic principles that help.

Radical Honesty

Radical honesty is the first essential condition for EFPs who want an enduring romantic relationship. They must be able to explain their limitations with utmost clarity so that their partners can make appropriate adjustments. Unfortunately I generally find these people radically *dishonest* when they first come to my office. They have learned from early childhood to avoid their electric fence at all costs, and that often means they must lie. When their parents tell them to do something that will make them unhappy, they don't do it. Instead, they lie about it and say they did it. Or, when their parents tell them not to do something that would make them happy, they do it anyway, and say they didn't. They get into the habit of being dishonest, because honesty often forces them to endure the pain of their electric fence.

But when the threat of the electric fence is removed, EFPs can become radically honest. In fact those I counsel usually tell me anything I want to know about them because they understand that I will not try to make them do anything unpleasant.

If they can be assured that there will be no demands that drag them into their fence, it's rather easy for them to be honest.

In every romantic relationship, partners should tell each other how they are likely to react to something that the other

> *Partners should tell each other how they*
> *are likely to react to something the other*
> *wants to do or wants them to do.*

wants to do or wants them to do. If applied to romantic relationships involving an EFP, that principle greatly reduces the chances of running into the electric fence. If you can be honest with each other about the nature of your problem, and if you have agreed that neither of you should suffer when you try to implement a solution, then you are in a position to solve the problem.

Prove That the Policy of Joint Agreement Works

Next, EFPs need to see how they can follow the Policy of Joint Agreement without running into their electric fence. The Policy of Joint Agreement is an EFP's friend. It protects the EFP from pain and guides him or her right down the middle of the road. Remember, this rule doesn't require you to do anything unless you are enthusiastic about it, so it will never lead you into your electric fence. Instead, it leads your partner past your fence and onto your path where he or she can become your enthusiastic friend and partner for life.

Everyone should be skilled in how to negotiate successfully in romantic relationships, but EFPs must be specially trained in this skill because the electric fence often interferes with the negotiating process itself. The very discussion of a problem and its alternatives can throw these people into their electric fence, making it seem almost impossible to negotiate. But I've trained thousands of EFPs to negotiate effectively.

Since EFPs usually have a very bad temper, one thing they must learn before they can become safe partners in a romantic relationship is anger management. In most cases I've witnessed, years of rage in response to their electric fence have

The Policy of Joint Agreement is an EFP's friend.

turned EFPs' angry outbursts into a habit that seems totally out of their control. Yet, with anger management training, these people are able to walk into their electric fence without ever hurting their partner. They must learn to get away from the electric fence as quickly as possible without reacting in panic or anger. And that's hard. But when practiced, a new habit is created that changes the angry outburst into an intelligent and responsible reaction.

In my earlier example, Beth created a scene at a restaurant on Valentine's Day because she had not learned how to manage her anger. Once she knew that their booth was her electric fence, a procedure for handling the situation should have been triggered. And she would have had to practice that procedure under calm conditions so that when the real electric fence showed up, she would be able to follow it almost instinctively. Otherwise, her panic and anger would dictate her reaction.

When I took scuba diving lessons, I had to practice emergency procedures that I would follow if I were to lose access to air from my tank. If my mouthpiece fell out of my mouth or if my tank ran low, I would immediately begin the plan that would save my life. But I didn't take the practice very seriously, and by the time I finished the course, these emergency procedures were not even close to being instinctive.

Sure enough, the day came when my tank ran out of air while I was 25 feet under water. I was trained to reach back and turn a valve that would give me another 5 minutes of reserve oxygen. I reached back but couldn't find the valve. Then I started to panic. I was taught another procedure for just that situation. If I would simply release my weight belt, the air in my vest would pop me right up to the surface. But in my panic, I forgot to release the weight belt. Instead, I did what I was taught *not* to do—struggle to get to the surface as best I could, weight belt and all.

I made it to the surface because I was only 25 feet under water, but if it had been 100 feet, I probably wouldn't be here to tell you about it. After that experience, I practiced emergency

Unless you have practiced your escape plan until it has become a habit, you won't follow it when the emergency arises.

procedures whenever I went on a dive. I learned that when in a state of panic, you simply cannot think rationally. Unless you have practiced your escape plan until it has become a habit, you won't follow it when the emergency arises. EFPs have the same problem. Unless they practice getting off their electric fence gracefully, they risk creating unnecessary problems for themselves and others.

If Beth had practiced anger management when she was calm, she would have learned how to state calmly but clearly that she was about to leave the situation that was creating her so much distress—the booth. Then she would have asked Doug if he would leave with her. If he were at all resistant, she would have left without him, without saying anything disrespectful or angry. Once outside the restaurant, she would have let him know that returning to the booth was not a possibility, but there were other possible solutions if he wanted to spend the evening with her. If he were to say anything disrespectful at that point, she would have practiced a procedure for that possibility. Without saying anything disrespectful or angry to Doug, she would have hailed a taxi and gone home by herself. You see, there was really nothing wrong with her taking the taxi home. Her problem was what she said before she got into the taxi.

In anger management training, people learn how to get out of a bad situation gracefully. They learn how to do it without disrespectful judgments or angry outbursts. Lots of training is needed, but the benefits are plentiful for those receiving the training as well as for all with whom they have contact.

Radical honesty and the Policy of Joint Agreement will minimize forays into the electric fence, but there is no way to stop them altogether. That's why anger management training is so important. EFPs must protect their partner at all costs, especially when their electric fence gets in their way. And anger management training helps an EFP become a safe partner in a romantic relationship.

Two EFPs

There's one last point I want to make before I leave this subject, and that has to do with the romantic relationship of two EFPs. What happens when two people with EFPs try to have a romantic relationship with each other?

It should be obvious to you by now that EFPs do not have the same flexibility that others have. Their electric fence greatly limits their choices in life. But if two EFPs try to form a romantic relationship, their combined limitations may make mutually enjoyable choices essentially impossible to find. So I usually discourage two EFPs from trying to form a romantic relationship.

This makes sense to most people, yet, because EFPs have such a common philosophical orientation to relationships (the Freeloader's philosophy), they tend to be drawn to each other

Pay close attention to how upset you or your partner becomes when either of you doesn't get your way.

like a moth is drawn to a lightbulb. And just like a moth, they usually get burned. An EFP needs someone with emotional flexibility—someone able to walk on their path without risk of walking into his or her own electric fence when there's a turn in the path. Instead, they usually end up with someone who is as emotionally limited as they are.

I've been able to show an EFP couple how to create a lifestyle that keeps them both from their electric fences, but it requires months, and sometimes years, of training. Their mutual inflexibility makes solutions to problems very difficult to discover. And patience, something usually lacking in EFPs, is often a key to that discovery. Solutions are much easier to find when at least one partner is flexible.

So if you are dating, pay close attention to how upset you or your partner becomes when either of you doesn't get your way. If either of you responds with panic or anger when something goes wrong, that person probably has an EFP that will limit his or her flexibility. If that's the case, my advice is for that person to practice anger management, radical honesty, and the Policy of Joint Agreement right away. If he or she can do it, your romantic relationship may turn out okay after all. But if you both have an EFP, you may find yourselves immobilized by the Policy of Joint Agreement. With four electric fences, you may find your choices so limiting that you'd be better off with someone else who is more flexible.

And at the risk of being redundant, whether you continue your relationship or not, you EFPs should undergo anger management training. You must learn to override your instinct to lash out at those around you when you hit your electric fence. Otherwise you'll never be able to negotiate successfully.

In chapters 11 and 12 of this book, I will explain to you in more detail how to negotiate with the Policy of Joint Agreement. If you or your partner has an Electric Fence Personality, take my advice when you come to those chapters. It may save your relationship if you follow it.

EFPs have problems in romantic relationships because of their inflexibility. But that's not the most important reason that their romantic relationships don't last. Their biggest problem is that they tend not to become Buyers. And I've found that regardless of their personality, unless couples eventually follow the Buyer's rule, a long-term romantic relationship won't succeed.

9

Compatibility Test or Curse?

Living Together before Marriage

The ideal sequence of agreements made during the development of a romantic relationship is the sequence that I made with Joyce—Freeloader to Renter and Renter to Buyer. But it's sad to note that an ever-increasing number of couples are going through a different sequence—Freeloader to Renter and Renter to Freeloader. These are the couples that have chosen to live together before marriage.

Living together before getting married is a common practice in today's world. People cite any number of seemingly practical reasons for doing so. But almost everyone who has studied these couples has come to the same conclusion. Marriages following cohabitation are almost inevitably doomed. I've seen it myself while counseling such couples. And I know why their marriages fail. In almost all cases, the problem in their marriage is that they never made a Buyer's agreement. Instead, when they married, one or both partners exchanged their Renter's agreement for a Freeloader's agreement. Read the letter below and you'll see what I mean.

Dear Dr. Harley,

I was married only four months ago after having been with my husband, Ed, for seven years, five of which we lived together. Since the wedding, he has been acting completely different.

Ed has turned our garage into his domain, complete with carpet, couches, appliances, and everything you would need in the perfect bachelor pad. He constantly has friends over and I am excluded. When he is not spending time in the garage, he is online or playing interactive computer games with his friends. He rarely comes to bed at the same time as me and just generally does not seem to be interested in sharing anything with me lately.

I understand that marriage is a huge change, but Ed never acted this way before. Why now? He is the one that really pushed getting married. I was very hesitant because of my parents' bad relationship. I even left him at one point three years ago because he was pressuring me so much. We discussed marriage at great length and both finally felt that it was the right time. So I do not understand his recent behavior.

Is this normal?

Becky

This letter is one of thousands I've received from people whose marriages crumbled after having lived together prior to marriage. It illustrates in a most vivid way what happens to most of these marriages. Instead of being more thoughtful and accommodating after making the commitment of marriage, people tend to become more thoughtless and self-centered.

Becky's husband, Ed, would not have dared transform the garage (and himself) before they got married because Becky would have left him if he had. Before marriage he took her feelings into account because if he had not, their relationship would have ended. They were both Renters.

Throughout their relationship, Ed put pressure on Becky to marry him so he could finally do what he pleased without fear of her leaving. He didn't explain that objective to her, of

Living together before marriage tends
to doom a romantic relationship.

course, but the way he pressured her made her so uncomfortable that she actually left him on one occasion. As I mentioned in chapter 7, a Renter tends to use control to get what he or she wants, and that control often leads to separation so the victim can avoid demands, disrespect, and anger.

Now that Ed is married to Becky, he thinks that she will stay with him in spite of what he does. He's become a Freeloader. But Becky won't put up with his Freeloading any more than Joyce put up with mine. Becky will probably divorce him, and theirs will join the vast majority of broken marriages that follow cohabitation.

Both my own experience of counseling cohabiting couples and research conducted by social scientists point to the same frightening conclusion—living together before marriage tends to doom a romantic relationship. Instead of making the relationship more solid, marriage tends to speed up its demise.

The risk of divorce for couples who lived together before marriage is 80 percent higher than the risk of divorce for non-cohabiting couples. In other words, those who live together before marriage are about twice as likely to divorce than those who did not live together. And the risk of divorce is *higher* than 80 percent if a couple lives together fewer than three years prior to marriage.[2]

One of the most common reasons couples live together before marrying is to test their compatibility. That sounds like a reasonable strategy to many people. But as it turns out, such a test appears to almost guarantee a divorce if they do marry.

David Hall and John Zhao conducted a study that controlled for factors that might have made divorce more likely among those who tend to cohabit (parental divorce, age at marriage, stepchildren, religion, and other factors). They showed that even when these effects are accounted for, cohabitation itself still accounts for a higher divorce rate. In other words, regardless of who you are, you are much more likely to divorce if you live together first.[3]

Alfred DeMaris and William MacDonald found that the unconventionality of those who live together does not explain their subsequent struggle when married. There is something about living together first that creates marital problems later. They write: "Despite a widespread public faith in premarital cohabitation as a testing ground for marital incompatibility, research to date indicates that cohabitors' marriages are less satisfactory and more unstable than those of non-cohabitors."[4]

The gist of current research is that if you live together before marriage, you will be fighting an uphill battle to create a happy and sustainable relationship.

Why Risk It?

The number of unmarried couples living together has increased dramatically over the past few decades, and I expect that it will continue to increase in the decades to come. Usually their rationale is simple: *By living together before marriage, we'll know how compatible we are.* Presumably, if a couple can get along living in the same apartment before marriage, they will be able to get along with each other after marriage.

That's a tempting argument. After all, a date tends to be artificial. Each person is up for the occasion, and they make a special effort to have a good time together. But marriage is quite different from dating. In marriage, couples are together when they're down too. Doesn't it make sense for a couple to live together for a while—just to see how they react to each other's down times? If they discover that they can't adjust when they live together, they don't have to go through the hassle of a divorce.

But life after marriage is considerably more complicated than life before marriage, particularly after children arrive.

> *Life after marriage is considerably more complicated than life before marriage.*

If couples that live together think that their lives will be essentially the same after marriage, they don't understand what marriage does to a couple, both positively and negatively. And while short-term solutions involving sacrifice may work for a while when living together, they ultimately destroy a romantic relationship, whether or not a couple eventually marries.

In my experience and in the reports I've just cited, the chances of a divorce after living together are huge, much higher than for couples that have not lived together prior to marriage. If living together were a good test of marital compatibility, the research should show opposite results. Couples living together should have stronger marriages. But they don't. They have weaker marriages. So what's going wrong here?

Why Doesn't It Work?

If you are unmarried and living with someone in a romantic relationship, or are contemplating doing so, ask yourself this question: Why did (or would) you choose to live with your partner instead of marrying him or her? Your answer is likely to have something to do with the fact that you (or your partner) were not yet ready to make an exclusive and permanent commitment. First, you wanted to see if you still felt the same about him or her after you cooked meals together, cleaned the apartment together, and slept together. And you probably wanted to see what married life would be like without the commitment of marriage.

Right now, you are testing each other to see if you are compatible. If either of you slips up, the relationship may end. That's because your commitment of living together is

Why did (or would) you choose to live with your partner instead of marrying him or her?

a tentative agreement: *As long as you behave yourself and keep me happy, I'll stick around.* It's a Renter's agreement.

You assume that your Renter's agreement will provide a valid test of how you will feel about each other, and how you will treat each other, when you are married. But that's only a valid assumption if you are willing to continue using your Renter's agreement after marriage. Under that agreement, if the conditions are not right, either of you can leave, marriage or no marriage. And if that's the way you want it, marriage really doesn't change anything. And it certainly doesn't commit you to much.

I assume, though, that marriage would mean something more to you than that. It would be a commitment not to leave each other when things get tough. But it's much more than a commitment not to leave. It's an agreement that you will take care of each other for life, regardless of life's ups and downs. You will stick with each other through thick and thin. In other words, the test is over. You have now made a final decision as to whom your life mate will be, and you commit yourself exclusively and permanently to that person's care, especially when it comes to meeting the intimate needs of a romantic relationship. Sounds like the Buyer's agreement, doesn't it?

But why should that marriage agreement ruin the relationships of those who have lived together first? What's wrong with a commitment to care for someone? It should make a relationship stronger, not weaker.

Becky's letter gives us the answer to that question. When she and Ed made their wedding vows, he heard her make a commitment to his care for life, regardless of what he did. While they were living together, he knew she had one foot out the door, and he did not want her to leave him. So he treated her with enough kindness to keep her around. But when she made the vow of marriage, he thought he was now free to be thoughtless. He didn't seem to pay much attention to the vow he made to care for her. On the day of their wedding, Ed traded his Renter's agreement in for a Freeloader's agreement.

Committed for Life

Most people want commitment after marriage. But there is considerable confusion as to what that commitment really means. Ed's idea of commitment was that Becky wouldn't leave him if he were thoughtless. Her commitment gave him the impression that he could do after marriage what he could not have done before marriage. And he may have gone so far as to assume that he was also committed not to leave her if she were thoughtless. In other words, his marriage vows didn't seem to have anything to do with a commitment to provide Becky care and thoughtfulness in marriage. It was simply a commitment not to leave her.

If care and thoughtfulness are not a commitment in marriage, the commitment not to leave doesn't make much sense.

The real commitment of marriage is not a commitment to stay regardless of how you are treated. It's a commitment to care for each other regardless of the circumstances you find yourselves in.

Why commit yourself to stay in an uncaring and thoughtless relationship? This crucial misunderstanding of commitment may fully explain why those who live together divorce so soon after marriage. They are making a commitment that no one in their right mind would keep.

The real commitment of marriage is not the one Ed thought he and Becky were making to each other. It's not a commitment to stay regardless of how you are treated. It's a commitment to care for each other regardless of the circumstances you find yourselves in. It means to "love and cherish each other in plenty and in want, in joy and in sorrow, in sickness and in health, as long as you both shall live." It's not about just sticking around. It's about loving and cherishing, especially under adverse conditions.

Marriage means that each spouse is committed to make a *greater* effort to care for each other than they were making before marriage, a greater effort to meet each other's intimate needs. But, unfortunately, couples who live together don't seem to care for each other after marriage as much as they did before marriage. They assume that they can get away with more. Instead of being motivated to do a better job, they tend to relax with the assumption that their spouse will put up with them, regardless of what they do. They believe that they don't need to do much to keep their spouse around after he or she makes that commitment.

So the commitment of marriage usually has an effect opposite to that which couples who live together hope it will have. Instead of encouraging each spouse to make a greater effort to care, it actually takes away the incentive to care. After all, when you live together, your success in caring for each other is the only thing keeping you together. If that care is taken away, you're history. But as Becky discovered, when care disappears after marriage, her commitment was expected to keep them together.

Is Renting Good Enough?

Not all couples who live together before marriage go through what Becky and Ed experienced. Ed went from being a Renter before marriage to a Freeloader after marriage. But many couples who cohabitate stay Renters after marriage. What happens to them?

Habits are hard to break, and couples who live together before marriage can get into the habit of following their month-to-month rental agreement. When a problem arises, they don't usually consider long-term solutions. Instead, they regularly rely on short-term solutions that involve sacrifice on the part of at least one partner. This strategy can work if problems are few and relatively simple to solve. But as soon as life becomes complicated, the way it eventually gets when children arrive, short-term strategies create long-term frustration and suffering when sacrifice is an essential part of the mix. So with the introduction of complex problems, such as raising children, marriages based on a Renter's agreement fall apart.

When those who live together before marriage finally decide to marry, it's not usually because they are willing to improve the way they have been solving problems. They marry because the arrangement has worked out well enough that they are willing to sign a long-term lease, so to speak. When I have an opportunity to explain to these couples the difference between short-term solutions that require one of them to sacrifice and long-term solutions that work well for both of

Some people speak the words of the Buyer's agreement when they make their wedding vows, but they continue to behave according to the terms of their Renter's agreement.

them, they are usually unwilling to give up their short-term solutions. They may speak the words of the Buyer's agreement at the time they make their wedding vows, but they continue to behave according to the terms of their Renter's agreement, willing to give sacrificially and expecting sacrifice in return. And as I have mentioned before, that usually leads to abuse.

Linda Waite found that couples who live together before marriage suffer three times the incidence of domestic violence that married couples suffer.[5] And my experience working with cases of domestic violence in marriage almost exclusively involves couples who lived together before they were married. So cohabiting not only leads to failed marriages, but it also leads to violence whether or not the couple ever marry. With the Renter's agreement in force, demands, disrespect, and anger are eventually the norm. Cohabiting couples don't look for solutions that make both of them happy. They look for solutions that make one person sacrifice for the happiness of the other. And if sacrifice is not forthcoming, punishment is inflicted.

But those who wait until after marriage to live together tend to experience a very low rate of violence and not much arguing. That's because they tend to be Buyers. They negotiate in a safe and enjoyable way, trying to find win-win solutions to their problems. They have not lived together under the terms

Build compatibility; don't test it.

of the month-to-month rental agreement. So they usually begin their life together with the assumption that they are there to make each other happy permanently, and their willingness and ability to change their habits to accommodate each other usually reflect that commitment. They want to build compatibility, not test it.

Marriage has a very positive effect on couples who date but do not live together, because after they take their vows, they tend to upgrade their care for each other. They make an effort to create a compatible lifestyle from day one. But marriage has a very negative effect on those who live together first because they tend to expect their partner to put up with anything they choose to do.

And avoiding marriage altogether does not save cohabiting couples. Instead, it leaves them with an increasingly abusive relationship. They may stay together a little longer when they don't marry, but their relationship usually becomes more violent. Make no mistake—cohabitation is a curse for marriage and an extremely dangerous way to be in a romantic relationship.

But the negative effect of having lived together before marriage can be overcome. Couples that cohabitate don't have to be destined to commit violent acts or end their relationship soon after marriage. All they must do is avoid the Renter's or Freeloader's agreement and become Buyers when they marry. In the remainder of this book, I'll explain how you can do just that. And if you follow my advice, you will overcome the curse of living together before marriage.

PART 3

The Buyer's Agreement—How Can You Make It Work?

10

Measuring Your State of Mind

Agreements You and Your Partner Make

So far I've explained what Buyers, Renters, and Freeloaders are all about and why the romantic relationships of Freeloaders and Renters are so disappointing and short-lived. I've also tried to convince you that the romantic relationship of Buyers is not only very fulfilling but also sustainable throughout life. Now you may be ready to take the plunge into giving the Buyer's agreement a shot. In this final section of the book, I will show you how you can see what it would be like to be a Buyer, without actually making a final commitment to an exclusive and permanent relationship.

Throughout this book, I've taken the position that what makes Buyers successful is not their commitment to an exclusive and permanent romantic relationship. Instead, I feel that it's their strategy to ensure the exclusiveness and permanence of their relationship. It's their willingness to make decisions that take each other's feelings into account that ultimately leads to a relationship where they want to be together for life.

If you want to be a Buyer, you have to follow the Buyer's rule—the Policy of Joint Agreement. That's the rule that

> *If you want to be a Buyer, you have*
> *to follow the Buyer's rule.*

guarantees the success of an exclusive and permanent romantic relationship. And you can try out that rule before you actually make an exclusive and permanent commitment to each other.

In the next two chapters, I'll show you how it feels to be a Buyer by teaching you how to follow the Buyer's rule. But first, I'd like you to understand your present state of mind regarding your romantic relationship. So in this chapter I will help you figure out what agreements you and your partner are using right now, and then encourage you to discuss why you have these agreements. By the time you finish this chapter, I hope you and your partner are both willing to try using the Buyer's rule to enhance your romantic relationship.

Assessing Where You Are Now

By now you get the gist of what defines a Buyer's agreement, a Renter's agreement, and a Freeloader's agreement. And you probably have an idea where you and your partner fit in respect to those categories. But I've designed the following questionnaire to make it a little easier for you to do so.

Test Yourself

The questions are all forced true-false questions, which means that even if you are not sure of your answer, you must respond either true or false. The blank in each question represents the name of your partner. But if you are not presently in a romantic relationship, you can still complete the questionnaire by imagining how you might respond when the next one comes along.

On a blank sheet of paper, write the numbers 1 through 30 to represent each question in the questionnaire. Then, beside each number, write either a T or F as your answer to that question. (The questionnaire is presented again in appendix A if you prefer to copy it in an enlarged form.) I'll show you how to score the questionnaire after you are finished.

Romantic Relationship Attitudes Questionnaire

1. If I am getting less than I need from _____, it's reasonable for me to expect him or her to sacrifice his or her happiness for my fulfillment.
2. Romantic relationships require a certain amount of give and take, but what I give to _____ should be worth what I take. In other words, I should be able to get out of this relationship what I put into it.
3. If we are right for each other, _____ will not want me to change.
4. I will be in an exclusive romantic relationship with _____ for life.
5. I am willing to sacrifice my happiness once in a while to satisfy _____ if he or she is willing to sacrifice his or her happiness once in a while to satisfy me.
6. I should do for _____ only whatever comes naturally to me.

7. Our romantic relationship is fatally flawed if _____ does not accept me as I am.

8. The goal of my romantic relationship with _____ is for us both to be happy and fulfilled with each other. As such, we must both learn to do everything with each other's interests and feelings in mind.

9. If _____ expects me to do something in return for his or her care of me, we are probably not right for each other.

10. If what I get in my romantic relationship with _____ isn't worth what I give, he or she should either give me more, or I should end the relationship to find someone who can give me more.

11. Solutions to the problems that _____ and I face should be long-term solutions that satisfy both of us.

12. _____ should not expect me to have a permanent romantic relationship with him or her.

13. Criticism from _____ should not cause me to try to change my behavior. It should cause me to consider ending our romantic relationship.

14. If _____ has a problem with some aspect of our romantic relationship, we should both work together to find a solution that we can permanently adopt.

15. Even though I am presently in an exclusive romantic relationship with _____, it's reasonable for me to compare him or her to others who may meet my needs more effectively.

16. _____ and I should learn how to make each other happy without sacrificing our own happiness to do it.

17. It's reasonable for _____ to expect me to do something in return for what he or she does for me.

18. The decisions that _____ and I make should make both of us happy and fulfilled.

19. If _____ criticizes me, it means that he or she is probably not right for me.

20. A short-term sacrifice may be necessary for me to learn a new habit or create a lifestyle change that accommodates _____. But if I am not eventually happy with the habit or lifestyle change, I should not continue to make the sacrifice.

21. If _____ criticizes me, he or she simply wants me to give more to compensate for what I am taking from him or her. So it's reasonable for me to give more to him or her if I feel that he or she is giving enough to compensate me for my effort.

22. If _____ wants me to do things for him or her that I do not feel like doing, he or she is probably wrong for me.

23. The mutual enjoyment and fulfillment that _____ and I share is more important than what either of us regards as fairness.

24. _____ may be right for me now but may be wrong for me later if he or she meets my needs now but fails to meet them at a later stage of my life.

25. When my needs or those of _____ change, an adjustment in habits and lifestyle should be made by both of us to accommodate the new needs so that our romantic relationship can be fulfilling to both of us throughout life.

26. _____ should not expect me to have an exclusive romantic relationship with him or her.

27. My romantic relationship with _____ should last as long as I feel it is fair.

28. I should be in an exclusive romantic relationship with _____ only as long as he or she is meeting my emotional needs.

29. If _____ were critical of me, it would indicate that an adjustment of my habits and lifestyle are required until the change would satisfy him or her.

30. If _____ is right for me, he or she will make me happy without my having to put much effort into making him or her happy.

Score the Questionnaire

After you and your partner have completed the questionnaire, add up the number of true answers to the following questions: 4, 8, 11, 14, 16, 18, 20, 23, 25, and 29.

Then, add up the number of true answers to these questions: 1, 2, 5, 10, 15, 17, 21, 24, 27, and 28.

Finally, add up the number of true answers to these questions: 3, 6, 7, 9, 12, 13, 19, 22, 26, and 30.

Which of the three groups of questions has the greatest number of true responses? If the first group has the largest number, the person answering the questions is probably a Buyer. If the second group has the largest number, he or she is probably a Renter. And if the third group has the largest number, he or she is probably a Freeloader.

If you have both answered these questions honestly, the results will give you a great deal of insight into the way you both approach your relationship. In fact the answer to each question should spark discussion, because each of them has something to do with how you will go about trying to solve problems that you will be facing.

You will probably have several true responses in more than one category. That will happen because none of us is entirely consistent in his or her beliefs. And it's also possible to have interpreted a question in a way I had not intended. That's why a discussion of each answer's meaning will be useful in making a final determination of the categories that best describe the beliefs of you and your partner.

For example, you may have answered true to question 7, indicating that you want to be accepted for who you are, yet you also may have answered true to question 29, indicating that you are willing to adjust to your partner's needs. A discussion of this apparent conflict may help you break out of a lingering resentment you feel whenever you are asked to accommodate your partner's feelings.

I haven't written this test as a foolproof determination as to whether someone is a Buyer, Renter, or Freeloader. If I had intended it to be part of a professional assessment, I would

Answer the questions with honesty and candor.

have included an unreliability scale (answering the same question differently), a lie scale (deliberate misrepresentations), a fake good scale (fudging the results to look good), and a fake bad scale (fudging the results to look bad). When used for professional assessment, psychological tests without these four added scales are probably not worth the paper they're written on. That's because people tend to misrepresent themselves when taking such tests, especially if a professional therapist is evaluating them.

I didn't include the extra questions in my questionnaire because I assume that you will approach it differently than you would if you were being professionally evaluated. Instead of answering the questions defensively, answer them with honesty and candor—you know each other well enough to determine the validity of your answers. Besides, the way you go about trying to resolve conflicts will be a dead giveaway if you're not being honest. Buyers, Renters, and Freeloaders have very distinctive approaches to solving problems in a romantic relationship. Freeloaders tend to ignore problems, Renters either give in or fight over them, and Buyers negotiate toward win-win solutions with care and respect for each other. If your test results conflict with your problem-solving style, you know your answers have not been completely honest.

Discuss Your Answers Honestly

As you and your partner go though your answers together, I encourage you to ask each other penetrating questions. And give each other honest answers so you can understand each other better and eliminate misinformation.

In fact, as you talk about this questionnaire, be *radically* honest with each other about everything. Dishonesty strangles a romantic relationship. To make your relationship everything you want it to be, you must lay your cards on the table and be

Ask each other penetrating questions.

honest about your thoughts, feelings, habits, likes, dislikes, personal history, daily activities, and plans for the future. When misinformation is part of the mix, you have little hope of making successful adjustments to each other. Dishonesty not only makes solutions hard to find, but it often leaves couples ignorant of the problems themselves.

There's another very important reason to be honest. Honesty tends to make our behavior more thoughtful. If we knew that everything we do and say would be televised and reviewed by all our friends, we would be far less likely to do many of the thoughtless things we do. We tend to be the most thoughtless when we assume our behavior will go undetected.

Honesty is the television camera in our lives. It records our actions and replays them to those around us. So when we're operating with this camera of honesty in place, we tend to be more thoughtful because we know we will reveal our behavior to our partner.

In an honest romantic relationship, thoughtless behavior is revealed and usually corrected before it becomes a habit. And bad habits are targeted for elimination when they are exposed to the light of day. That's because each partner tries harder to avoid thoughtless behavior when they both know about it. And when an innocent act happens to offend a partner, honesty makes it clear that it should not be repeated in the future.

Honesty helps keep a couple from drifting into incompatibility. As incompatible behavior is revealed, it can be changed. But if this behavior remains hidden, it is left to grow out of control. That's why it's critical for you to be radically honest with each other if you want your relationship to grow in compatibility.

Discovering Where You've Been

When a couple first sees me for counseling, I have them complete my Personal History Questionnaire, which systematically reviews many of the significant events of their past. I ask them to share their answers with each other and feel free to ask any questions that are triggered by them.

You and your partner should take the same opportunity to learn about each other's past. You will find a copy of the Personal History Questionnaire in appendix B. Make two enlarged (8½ x 11) copies, one for each of you.

At the beginning of the Personal History Questionnaire, there is a reminder to be radically honest when answering the questions. My *Rule of Honesty for Successful Marriage* is printed there, and I encourage both of you to agree to it before you complete the questionnaire.

The questionnaire covers your health history, family history, educational history, vocational history, religious history, opposite-sex relationship history, sexual history, personal assessment, and goals for personal improvement. It's very likely that some of the information you provide will be facts you've never known about each other.

If there is information that you consider too personal to reveal, I encourage you not to answer the question until you have gained a greater trust in each other. And the answers should be treated with utmost confidence. Professional psychologists who use similar questionnaires are ethically bound never to reveal their contents without the person's written permission. You should treat each other's personal information with the same respect.

Once you've both completed the questionnaire, write a short personal history of each other. Your completed questionnaires will give you basic information, and you can fill in the

Treat each other's personal information
with utmost respect and sensitivity.

gaps by asking each other questions while writing the reports. While one of you asks questions and types the history, the other simply answers the questions as honestly as possible. Then switch roles so that histories are written for both of you.

These short personal histories will not only help you know each other and understand each other better, they will also be invaluable to family members who want to know something about your lives. But be sure to get your partner's permission before revealing his or her history to anyone else. Don't include references to sexual history or anything else that either of you would consider embarrassing. Treat each other's personal information with utmost respect and sensitivity.

Ready to Become Buyers?

Now that you know more about each other's past and about where you stand now, I have an important question to ask: Where do you want to go from here?

There comes a time in most romantic relationships when at least one partner wants to make it permanent. That's partly due to practical considerations, such as wanting to end the search for a partner, to settle down, and to raise a family. To be honest, I was greatly relieved when Joyce and I were married because it ended the indignity of rejection and the awkwardness of rejecting.

But the most important reason Joyce and I married was that we were very much in love. We couldn't imagine going though life without each other. Love is a feeling of such incredible attraction to someone of the opposite sex that you find the person irresistible. People feel that way when their most important emotional needs have been met, even if it's only for a day. But if their needs are being met consistently, that feeling of love seems to be something that will last forever. So those in love have a natural desire to make the relationship permanent.

Most people are sophisticated enough these days to know that the feeling of love comes and goes in just about every romantic relationship. Couples usually don't tie the knot right after the love bug bites—they usually wait a while to see if it will last. And then there are some who don't want to make the relationship permanent regardless of how much in love they are—or how long they've been in love. They have seen what marriage, and subsequent divorce, has done to their parents, their friends, and even themselves. So when they are in love, they just want to savor the moment and hope it lasts for a while.

Many of these people decide that it's safer just living together than it is to marry. That way they can have many of the advantages of marriage without the risks. But as I mentioned in the last chapter, when a couple lives together before marriage, they are in the most dangerous romantic relationship of all. Not only does it tend to ruin any hope of a successful marriage later on, but it also creates the greatest risk for domestic violence. It's a very foolish alternative to marriage, yet people are doing it in ever-greater numbers.

Marriage is not what it used to be, that's for sure. Instead of a permanent romantic relationship where two people in love join together to raise a family, for most people it has become one of many temporary romantic relationships. Mar-

There is a formula for success in marriage.

riages followed by divorce have created social, emotional, and economic upheaval for many people. If you have ever been in a bad marriage and were subsequently divorced, you will count it among your very worst experiences in life. And you won't be alone. So it's no wonder people are reluctant to marry these days. With the threat of divorce looming over their heads, people search for ways to have romantic relationships without marriage—or divorce.

But what if you could be assured of a lifetime of love without the threat of divorce? Would marriage be more appealing then? That's the way marriage is supposed to be and the way it is for Joyce and me as well as for millions of other couples.

There *is* a formula for success in marriage. I've been alluding to it throughout this book. It's what Buyers do for each other when they are in a romantic relationship. So if you would like your love for each other to be permanent—and avoid the risk of divorce after you marry—all you need to do is become Buyers.

Quite a few beliefs come together to define a Buyer—exclusivity (avoiding all other romantic relationships) and permanence (regarding the romantic relationship as a life-long commitment) being the most obvious. But the desire and willingness to search for win-win solutions to all problems is ultimately what makes the Buyer's agreement so effective. As Buyers, a couple creates habits and a lifestyle that make them both happy and avoid making either of them unhappy. When that's accomplished in a romantic relationship, there's no point to either having another romantic relationship or ending the relationship. The commitment to an exclusive and permanent relationship is easy to keep.

So my focus of attention for the remainder of this book will not be trying to convince you that you should be committed to exclusiveness and permanence. I'm not sure I could do that effectively, especially after some of the experiences you may have had in past relationships. But I think I *can* convert you into acting like a Buyer by encouraging you to change your behavior. And that, in turn, will encourage you to make the Buyer's commitment on the day you marry.

Remember what I said in chapter 5 about psychologist Leon Festinger and his theory of cognitive dissonance? It turns out that it's easier to change your attitudes and beliefs when your behavior is consistent with them. Right now, you are probably acting like a Freeloader or Renter. If I were to try to convince both of you to become exclusively and permanently commit-ted, like a Buyer, your Freeloading or Renting habits would quickly destroy the reasonableness of that commitment.

So I'd like to encourage you and your partner to become Buyers by first changing your habits. Once your habits have changed, a commitment to be exclusive and permanent lovers will make more sense to you.

A crucial step in becoming a Buyer is to follow the Buyer's rule, the Policy of Joint Agreement—never do anything without an enthusiastic agreement between you and your partner.

Become Buyers by first changing your habits.

I'll talk about that more in the next chapter. But for now, I'll encourage you to practice the rule, not as a permanent commitment, but rather as an experiment to see if it really works. You'll find that the longer you use it to make your decisions, the happier you will be in your relationship, the more compatible you'll become, and the more secure your love for each other will be.

To a Freeloader or Renter, the Policy of Joint Agreement makes no sense at all. It makes sense only to Buyers. But even if you are a Freeloader or Renter, you can follow the rule for a while, just to see what it would be like to be a Buyer. The rule requires no changes in your beliefs or attitudes for it to work. In fact you don't even have to believe it will work. All you have to do is follow the Policy and let the results speak for themselves.

So let's give it a try!

11

Adopting the Buyer's Strategy

The Policy of Joint Agreement

Just because a relationship is exclusive and permanent doesn't mean it's desirable. In fact, if it is painful for either partner, a lifelong commitment is a lifelong mistake.

It makes no sense for Freeloaders to be exclusively and permanently committed to each other. Their unwillingness to be thoughtful makes even the best compatibility and chemistry wither in the face of one selfish act after another. In my chapter on Freeloaders, Becky's husband, Ed, gave you a glimpse of what Freeloaders are really all about. They totally ignore the interests of their partner. Why be exclusively and permanently committed to someone like Ed?

And in many ways, Renters are worse off than Freeloaders. Their way of solving problems—fighting and demanding sacrifice—creates a dreadful lifestyle. Instead of both partners

The Policy of Joint Agreement

Never do anything without an enthusiastic agreement between you and your partner.

being happy, one is usually unhappy. Why would a couple want to be exclusively and permanently committed under those conditions?

If your romantic relationship is to succeed, you must do more than commit exclusively and permanently. You must also commit to creating mutual fulfillment and avoiding individual suffering. That's why I urge couples to focus on their care and consideration for each other instead of their exclusive and permanent commitment.

Don't get me wrong. I'm definitely in favor of an exclusive and permanent commitment between lovers. I encourage marriage and discourage divorce. It's just that without mutual care, such a commitment usually doesn't hold up over time.

So I'd like to try to convert you and your partner into Buyers the same way I try to convert the couples I've counseled. First, I want you to learn how to care for each other the way Buyers care for each other. Then, because your relationship will be mutually enjoyable, it will be much easier for you to make a commitment to care for each other exclusively and permanently as Buyers when you marry.

Your most important tool for doing this is the Policy of Joint Agreement: *Never do anything without enthusiastic agreement between you and your partner*. By following this rule, you will begin to think of yourselves as a bonded unit instead of two disinterested individuals.

If your relationship is going to be valuable to both you and your partner, you must consider both your interests *and* your partner's interests whenever you make a decision. One of you should not gain at the other's expense, even willingly, because if either of you suffers, your relationship will suffer. And if you both care about each other, neither of you will want the other to suffer.

Your Giver and Taker tempt you to sacrifice and expect

You must consider both your interests and your partner's interests.

sacrifice from each other, yet sacrificing jeopardizes the health of your relationship. So you need a rule to protect you from the instinctive yet destructive compromises your Giver and Taker urge you to make. And the Policy of Joint Agreement is that rule.

It will help you tear down all the barriers that prevent Freeloaders and Renters from experiencing a successful and sustainable romantic relationship. And once those barriers are torn down, an exclusive and permanent relationship will make sense to you.

A Policy Worth Trying

So what do you think of this rule? Let me guess.

If you are a Freeloader, you probably think this rule is crazy. Most Freeloaders do. After all, if you accept each other unconditionally, why should you have to change your plans just to make the relationship work? If either partner objects to what the other intends to do, it's not an indication that you should do something else. It's evidence that you are not right for each other.

If you're a Renter, you may be a little less severe in your judgment. Renters don't usually reject this rule outright. But they don't wholeheartedly embrace it either. Their Giver likes the way it protects their partner by requiring the partner's enthusiastic agreement, and their Taker likes the part that requires their own enthusiastic agreement before their partner does anything. But on the other hand, their Giver thinks

The difference between reluctant agreement and enthusiastic agreement is just a little more thoughtfulness—and creativity.

they are being selfish when they don't do whatever it takes to make their partner happy, even if doing it makes them unhappy. And their Taker thinks they are just plain dumb to let their partner's lack of enthusiasm prevent them from doing whatever makes them happy. So Renters have a very mixed reaction that generally leads to a very inconsistent application of the rule.

Renters are usually dominated by their Takers by the time I see them. So they tend to like the Policy of Joint Agreement when it's applied to their partner, but they don't like it when it's applied to themselves. If you are a Renter, you'll probably have a similar reaction, seeing the policy's value when your partner is being thoughtless but wanting to ignore it when you are being thoughtless.

Only if you're a Buyer will you immediately see the sense in this rule, because it's something you've wanted to do all along. Since Buyers already believe in win-win solutions to problems, they like the idea of making decisions together and are intrigued with the challenge of finding an "enthusiastic" agreement. They can see that the difference between reluctant agreement and enthusiastic agreement is just a little more thoughtfulness—and creativity.

But you're probably *not* a Buyer, especially if you are not yet married. You're probably a Renter or maybe even a Freeloader, which means it's safe to assume that your reaction to this rule is at least somewhat negative. In spite of your negative reaction, however, I'd like to challenge you to follow the rule anyway, at least for a while. Because, whether you are a Buyer, Renter, or Freeloader, this policy will help you connect to your partner's feelings, especially when you don't feel like doing so. And if you both follow it, you'll find yourselves becoming increasingly compatible.

That's what compatibility is all about—building a way of life that is comfortable for both partners. When two people

Compatibility is about building a way of life that is comfortable for both partners.

create a lifestyle that they each enjoy and appreciate, they build compatibility into their romantic relationship. And with compatibility, they avoid becoming each other's worst nightmare and learn how to meet each other's emotional needs.

Anyone Can Do It—At Least for a While

When I first see a couple that are both Freeloaders, they are living their lives as if the other hardly exists—making thoughtless decisions regularly because they often don't care how the other feels. As a result, when I introduce the Policy of Joint Agreement to them, it seems totally irrational. They have created so many inconsiderate habits that the policy threatens their entire way of life.

In spite of their reservations, though, they are usually willing to give the rule a very short-term test, and that's all I usually need to get them started on the right track. At first, the Policy of Joint Agreement seems impossible to follow because they do not want to abandon their thoughtless and insensitive habits and activities. However, once they start to follow the rule, it becomes easier and easier to come to an agreement as they replace thoughtless habits with those that take each other's feelings into account. As they watch their relationship turn into one that is mutually fulfilling, I'm usually able to convert them from their Freeloader's agreement to a Buyer's agreement. And if Freeloaders can do it, anyone can.

A Team Effort

The Policy of Joint Agreement prevents either of you from making unilateral decisions about anything, so you must discuss every decision you make before action can be taken. Once the question "How do you feel about what I would like

The word enthusiastic should get your attention.

to do?" is asked, if the reaction is not enthusiastic, you have the choice of either abandoning the entire idea or trying to discover alternative ways of making it possible. And that's where negotiation begins. With practice, you can both become experts at getting what you need in ways that create a mutual and enthusiastic agreement.

The word *enthusiastic* should get your attention. It's a Taker's word because your Taker will be enthusiastic about an agreement that's in your own best interest. And your partner's Taker will be enthusiastic about an agreement in his or her best interest. Your Taker is your advocate. It wants the best for you and usually knows what will make you happy.

So when you are enthusiastic about something, it means that your Taker has given it the stamp of approval.

Your Giver, on the other hand, never shows much enthusiasm for what it encourages you to do, although it does provide "reluctant" agreement when you are willing to help sacrificially. I want you to avoid the self-sacrificing agreements proposed by your Giver, and anything short of a mutually enthusiastic agreement may not be in your best interest.

Since your agreements should be good for both of you, I want you to use one of the most reliable tests—your Takers' stamp of approval of mutual enthusiasm. Without it, you should both keep searching for better alternatives.

How Does It Work?

How does this policy work out in real life? To demonstrate its usefulness, let's look at three couples and their problem-solving strategies.

Couple A

Tom and Mary do not discuss their plans with each other, much less agree. They just go ahead and do whatever they feel like doing with no consideration whatsoever for each other's feelings. If Tom wants to go out with his friends on weekends, he does so, without asking Mary how she would feel about it. She also makes her plans without consulting with Tom. She rarely knows exactly where he is, and he doesn't know her whereabouts either.

Tom and Mary have been dating for a while but have become increasingly incompatible, developing a lifestyle and personal habits that ignore each other's feelings. For them, just asking the question "How do you feel about what I would like to do?" is inconceivable. They don't really care how the other one feels. They are Freeloaders.

Way back in the beginning of their relationship, they enjoyed each other's company and were in love with each other. But their Freeloading ways completely destroyed that love. In fact Mary doesn't even know what it was she first saw in Tom that was attractive.

Couple B

Rick and Janet use a somewhat better decision-making strategy. They discuss their plans with each other and consider how they would affect the other. But they both expect sacrifice. So when one expresses reservations about what the other is planning, the issue becomes one of who cares enough to sacrifice his or her own interests.

For instance, there was a business trip that Rick wanted to take to improve his standing with his company, but it coincided with Janet's birthday. He talked it over with her, and she registered her displeasure with his being gone on her birthday. He argued that if she cared about him, she would support his career opportunities. She replied that if he cared about her, he would postpone the trip to be with her on her birthday. He decided to go on the trip anyway.

Janet was offered a community leadership position that would keep her busy most evenings and weekends. Rick explained how that would keep them from getting together, since that was the only time they could date. But she argued that if he cared about her, he would support her community ambitions. She accepted the offer.

To the extent that they are expecting each other to sacrifice their feelings and interests, they are building an incompatible lifestyle. Discussing their plans helps them understand each other, and they do try to accommodate each other once in a while with that understanding. For example, when Rick learned that Janet objected to a certain aftershave lotion that he bought, he stopped using it. But because their thoughtfulness

If you expect each other to sacrifice feelings and interests, you are building an incompatible lifestyle.

is inconsistent, their feelings are often hurt, and that rouses their Takers, plunging them into one argument after another. They are Renters.

Rick and Janet both admit that they are losing passion in their relationship. It took them longer to lose it than it took Tom and Mary, but their failure to make appropriate adjustments to each other's feelings has taken its toll. A counselor once told them that the feeling of passion in a relationship should not be expected to continue indefinitely, that they had entered a more "mature" and less passionate stage. But that counselor's advice wasn't based on fact. It was based on the failure of his own romantic relationships. Rick's and Janet's loss of passion is a warning that they have entered the second and final stage of their Renter's relationship—they hurt each other instead of care for each other. If they don't switch to the Buyer's agreement soon, they will have no choice but to end their relationship to escape increasing abuse.

Couple C

Dan and Carla go one step further. They do not do anything unless there is at least *reluctant* agreement. Their Givers try to influence them to "agree," even when it is not in their best interest to do so. Their hearts are in the right place, but their unselfish approach actually encourages incompatibility.

One Monday evening, Dan wanted to watch football with one of his friends and invited Carla to go with him. She not only refused, but she let him know that she didn't even want him to go. She wanted him to spend the evening with her, but she didn't want to watch football with his friends. He reluctantly agreed to go out with her to see a movie that evening, but he was very resentful. All evening he was quiet, thinking about the game. By the time the evening was over, Carla wished she had agreed to let him go, because he was so unpleasant to be around.

Dan was able to override his Taker's wishes to watch football but did not take the crucial next step of finding an alternative that would make him just as happy. So his Taker protested vigorously. And Dan got his Taker's message loud

Most of us view sacrifice as a noble thing, but it's really very risky in a romantic relationship.

and clear. Before the evening was over, he flew into a rage over some insignificant issue. Three days later, when he was telling me about the incident, he had forgotten what had made him lose his temper, but he sure remembered having given up watching *Monday Night Football* with his friends.

Reluctant agreement *seems* to be a satisfactory solution for many couples. Most of us view personal sacrifice as a noble thing, giving up our well-being for the good of others—but it's really very risky in a romantic relationship. When you reluctantly agree to some course of action with your partner, it usually means that he or she will be happy at your expense. That leads you to expect to gain at your partner's expense. If a decision is not in the best interest of *both* of you, it is not in the best interest of your romantic relationship.

Dan and Carla were very close to following the Policy of Joint Agreement. As a result, their romantic relationship, and their love for each other, was still intact when I first met them. When Dan lost his temper, he realized he had hurt Carla, something he had promised her he would not do, and that's what triggered their appointment with me.

The Place of Sacrifice

Dan's problem in resolving his *Monday Night Football* conflict was his willingness to sacrifice his own feelings for Carla's feelings. That ultimately led to resentment and then to an angry outburst. But isn't sacrifice helpful in a romantic relationship, at least some of the time?

When I discussed the approach Buyers take to the issue of sacrifice in chapter 4, I noted that sacrifice can make sense when it helps us achieve our own personal long-term objectives. And you *can* sacrifice under the terms of the Policy of Joint Agreement. So I'm not saying that you should never sacrifice in a romantic relationship. We have all wisely sacrificed our own short-term interests for the sake of a long-term interest. Not

I'm not saying that you should never sacrifice, but be cautious about sacrifice.

every decision we make will or should bring immediate benefit. For example, I went through quite a bit of self-sacrifice when I earned a PhD in psychology. It was no fun, I assure you. Yet my Taker was with me in this plan because it could see future value in my decision. Joyce and I both were in enthusiastic agreement regarding my education, and because of that I had no reason to feel resentment toward her, even though it was a sacrifice for me.

But if I had felt that my education benefited only Joyce, and if she had tried to force me to complete my degree, it would have been a different story. I'd probably still be complaining about what she put me through, even if it had turned out to be in my own best interest.

My education wasn't a cakewalk for Joyce either. If I had been in graduate school without her enthusiastic agreement, she would continue to resent to this very day the sacrifices she made on my behalf. But because Joyce's Taker viewed my education as being in her best interest, she enthusiastically supported the decision for me to complete my degree.

On completing my PhD degree, I was offered an opportunity to continue my education in a program that would have led to a medical degree. But Joyce's sacrifice had reached its limit, and she let me know that she would not be enthusiastic about any further education. So that's where my formal education ended. If I had gone ahead with plans for a medical degree, Joyce would still remember the experience as among the worst in her life—not just because it would have meant

Your Taker needs to be enthusiastic about every decision.

further sacrifice on her part but because it would have meant my career would have been more important to me than her feelings. Our marriage may not have ended, but our romantic relationship would likely have been finished if I had made that choice.

What I'm saying is that your Taker needs to be enthusiastic about *every* decision. That doesn't rule out short-term sacrifice, though, because your Taker can be enthusiastic about some forms of sacrifice, if they're in your long-term interest. But when you agree to something reluctantly, it means you are sacrificing with no personal gain in sight. You are doing it for someone else's gain. That's why your Taker usually tries to sabotage any agreement you have made reluctantly. Have you ever noticed that agreements requiring sacrifice by either you or your partner are difficult to implement? It's your Taker trying to gum up the works.

So let's evaluate the three alternatives to the Policy of Joint Agreement illustrated in couples A, B, and C. I think we would all agree that Tom and Mary, our first couple, are in deep trouble as they pass each other like ships in the night. Their Freeloader strategy of self-centered decision making did not sustain their romantic relationship very long.

Rick and Janet, couple B, have taken a step in the right direction by discussing their feelings and interests with each other, but they're in trouble too. They have allowed thoughtlessness to come between them, and that's ruined their romantic relationship. Their Renter's strategy doesn't create solutions to problems—it eventually creates fights. With problems mounting and their relationship becoming increasingly adversarial, it can't last much longer.

Dan and Carla's strategy of reluctant agreement is a vast improvement over the way couples A and B try to solve problems, but they don't have the answer either. Instead of creating compatibility, they miss the mark. Their romantic relationship seems to be secure, yet both find themselves uncomfortable with the direction their relationship is taking. Why would Dan prefer to be with his friends instead of spending the evening alone with Carla? Something is missing.

What's missing is the wisdom of their Takers. Their reluctant agreement creates decisions that leave their Takers out of the final decision, and when that happens, Takers create a scene. The only way for them to be completely happy with the decision they make is to negotiate until there's an *enthusiastic* agreement between them. That insures the Taker's participation in those decisions. When that happens, it can truly be said that they live in harmony with each other. They would then be using the Buyer's strategy.

How Do You Feel About . . .

As soon as you and your partner adopt the Policy of Joint Agreement to guide you in your romantic relationship, you will have taken a giant step forward in your ability to negoti-

The Policy of Joint Agreement forces you to be considerate, especially when you don't feel like it.

ate because you will be forced to ask each other the question, "How do you feel about what I would like to do?" Prior to your consideration of this policy, that question may not have come up very often. You have probably made many of your decisions unilaterally, without any consideration for each other's feelings. But the Policy of Joint Agreement *forces* you to be considerate, especially when you don't feel like it.

And when you ask the question, "How do you feel about what I would like to do?" you take the first step in negotiation, raising the issue and seeking agreement before any action is taken.

Your Giver doesn't care how you feel about your partner's behavior, as long as he or she is having fun doing it. And your Taker doesn't care about how your partner feels about your behavior, as long as you do it without his or her interference. The question, "How do you feel?" is completely foreign to the way either of them approach a problem.

So at first, the question will seem very strange, even humorous, to you. That's because you don't instinctively think in those terms, especially in a romantic relationship. Yet the question is at the very core of every negotiation, and you must force yourselves to ask it if you want your relationship to thrive.

While the question, "How would you feel?" gets negotiation started and the Policy of Joint Agreement is your final goal (enthusiastic agreement), you may be at a loss to know what should go on in between. In other words, how do you arrive at an enthusiastic agreement?

Dan and Carla (couple C) needed an effective negotiating procedure when the *Monday Night Football* issue came up. Dan wanted to go out to watch television with his friends and wanted Carla to join him. Carla wanted to be with him but didn't want to watch football with his friends. She wanted to see a movie instead. Because they were not used to negotiating for an enthusiastic agreement, those were the only two alternatives from which they could choose. And either choice would cause one of them to end up feeling resentful.

If you are like Dan and Carla and have not been in the habit of negotiating for an enthusiastic agreement, I suggest you begin formally and practice the steps that I suggest in the next chapter. It may be awkward and frustrating for you at first. But when you and your partner eventually become comfortable negotiating with each other, it won't seem so formal to you and won't be frustrating. In fact most of the time you will be negotiating on the run, taking as little as a few minutes to come to an enthusiastic agreement. If you keep practicing, eventually you will reach those wise decisions, which Dan and Carla should have made, with very little effort.

Following the Policy of Joint Agreement will insulate you from many of the destructive forces that ruin romantic relationships. And it will also help you learn to meet each other's needs in ways that are mutually fulfilling and enjoyable. If you follow this policy and meet each other's needs, you'll fall in love and stay in love with each other. That's the most powerful incentive of all for following this policy.

12

Bargaining with Finesse

Guidelines for Successful Negotiation

Let's begin with the assumption that you have taken the first
step toward following the Policy of Joint Agreement—you
have asked your partner how he or she would feel about meeting one of your unmet needs or about overcoming a thoughtless
habit that is bothering you or about "letting" you do something
you've had your heart set on doing for the last six months.
Then, to your dismay, your partner indicates that he or she is
not "enthusiastic" about whatever it is you want.

Chances are that in the past you have responded to conflicts
like this in one of three ways: (1) ignoring your own feelings and doing it your partner's way—the Giver's solution,
(2) ignoring your partner's feelings and doing it your way—
the Taker's solution, or (3) ignoring the problem entirely—
the Freeloader's solution. Successful negotiation, however,

requires something very different—finding a way to resolve the conflict that simultaneously takes into account both your feelings and those of your partner. That's the Buyer's solution.

Expert negotiators make a living discovering win-win solutions to business and political problems. And almost all of them follow a simple plan for success. I suggest you follow the same plan whenever you and your partner are not in enthusiastic agreement. The following Four Guidelines for Successful Negotiation outline this plan.

Guideline 1

Set ground rules to make negotiation pleasant and safe.
Most couples view negotiation as a trip to the torture chamber. That's because their efforts are usually fruitless, and they come away from the experience battered and bruised. Who wants to negotiate when it brings nothing but disappointment and pain?

So before you begin to negotiate, set some basic ground rules to make sure that you both enjoy the experience. Why? Because you tend to repeat activities that you like and avoid those you don't like. Since you should negotiate whenever a conflict arises, it should be as enjoyable as possible so that you will make it a regular part of your life.

To be certain that you will have a pleasant and safe negotiating environment, I suggest three ground rules.

Ground Rule 1: *Try to be pleasant and cheerful throughout negotiations*. It's fairly easy to start discussing an issue while in a good mood. But negotiations can open a can of worms, so be prepared for negative emotional reactions. Your partner may begin to feel uncomfortable about something you say. In fact he or she may suddenly inform you that there will be no further discussion.

I know how upset and defensive couples can become when they first tell each other how they feel about the way they have been treated. That's why I first coach them individually to prepare them for negative comments. I simply tell them what I am telling you—try to be as positive and cheerful as you can be, especially if your partner says something that offends you.

Ground Rule 2: *Put safety first*. Don't make demands, show disrespect, or become angry when you negotiate, even if your partner makes demands, shows disrespect, or becomes angry with you. Once the cat is out of the bag and you have told your partner what is bothering you or what you want, you have entered one of the most dangerous phases of negotiation. If your partner's initial reaction hurts your feelings, you are tempted to retaliate. Your Taker is very persuasive at this point, and unless you make a special effort to resist its advice, your negotiation will turn into an argument. But if you can keep each other safe, you will be able to use your intelligence to help you make the changes you both need. Nothing can prevent you from feeling like making demands or being disrespectful of your spouse's opinions or even becoming angry. But you can avoid saying anything that is demanding, disrespectful, or angry. Keep demands, disrespect, and anger to yourself.

Ground Rule 3: *If you reach an impasse and don't seem to be getting anywhere, or if one of you is starting to make demands, show disrespect, or become angry, stop negotiating and come back to the issue later*. Just because you can't resolve a problem at a particular point in time doesn't mean you can't find an intelligent solution in the future. Don't let an impasse prevent you from giving yourself a chance to think about the issue. Let it incubate for a while, and you'll be amazed what your mind can do when the issue comes up later.

If your negotiation turns sour, and one of you succumbs to the temptation of the Taker with a demand, a disrespectful judgment, or an angry outburst, end the discussion by changing the subject to something more pleasant. After a brief pause, your partner may apologize and wish to return to the subject that was so upsetting. But don't go back into the minefield until it has been swept clear of mines. The mines, of course, are demands, disrespect, and anger, and you should address those issues before you begin negotiating again. You can't negotiate successfully if your Takers' destructive instincts control your discussion.

Guideline 2

Identify the problem from both perspectives. Once you have set ground rules that guarantee a safe and enjoyable discussion, you are ready to negotiate. But where do you begin? First, you must understand the problem from the perspectives of both you and your partner.

Most couples try to resolve a conflict without doing their homework. They don't fully understand the conflict itself, nor do they understand each other's perspectives. In many cases, they are not even sure what they really want or what they're enthusiastically willing to give.

One of the responsibilities of a counselor is to help couples clarify the issues that separate them. I'm amazed at how often the clarification itself solves the problem. "Oh, that's what we've been fighting about!" many couples have said to me. And once they understand the issue and each other's perspective, they realize that the conflict is not as serious as they thought. Or when the issue is clarified, the solution is immediately apparent and the conflict is resolved.

Respect is the key to success in this phase of negotiation. Once the issue has been identified and you hear each other's perspective, it is extremely important to avoid trying to straighten each other out. Remember that your goal is *enthusiastic* agreement, and there is no way you will be enthusiastic if you reject each other's perspective. In fact the only way

Respect is the key to success in
this phase of negotiation.

you will reach an enthusiastic agreement is if you come up with a solution that accommodates each other's perspective.

It's so much easier to negotiate the right way when your goal is enthusiastic agreement. It eliminates all the strategies that attempt to wear each other down with abuse. You may as well forget about making demands, because they never lead to an enthusiastic agreement. The same can be said for making disrespectful judgments and having angry outbursts. If you are looking for real solutions to your problems, you will find them only in whatever yields an enthusiastic agreement.

But when I take demands, disrespect, and anger away from some couples, they are left feeling hopeless about resolving their conflicts. They don't know how to discuss an issue if they can't demand, show disrespect, or express their anger. It's as if the only way they know how to communicate in a relationship is through some form of abuse. Is that true of you and your partner?

If so, remember that with practice you will begin to feel more comfortable approaching every conflict with the goal of enthusiastic agreement. You will learn to ask each other questions to gain a fuller understanding of what it would take to make each other happy. And when you think you have the information you need to consider win-win solutions, you are ready for the next guideline.

Guideline 3

Brainstorm with abandon. You've set the ground rules. You've identified the conflict from each other's perspective. Now you're ready for the creative part—looking for solutions that you think will make you both happy. I know that can seem impossible if you and your partner have drifted into incompatibility. But the climb to compatibility has to start somewhere, and if you put your minds to it, you'll think of options that please you both.

The secret to understanding your partner is to try to think like your partner's Taker thinks. It's easy to appeal to your partner's Giver. *If she really loves me, she'll let me do this.*

Quantity is often more important than quality.

Or, *he'll be thoughtful enough to agree with that, I'm sure.* But lasting peace must be forged with your partner's Taker, so your solutions must appeal to your partner's most selfish instincts. At the same time, they must also appeal to your own selfish instincts.

When you brainstorm, quantity is often more important than quality. Let your minds run wild; go with just about any thought that might satisfy both of your Takers. If you let your creativity run free, you are more likely to find a lasting solution.

Carry a pad of paper or a pocket notebook with you so you can write down ideas as you think of them throughout the day. Some problems may require days of thought and pages of ideas. But keep in mind your goal—a solution that will appeal to both of your Takers.

Resist one type of solution that your Giver and Taker may suggest—the I'll-let-you-do-what-you-want-this-time-if-you-let-me-do-what-I-want-next-time solution. That's the Renter's solution that encourages you to alternate sacrificing for each other.

For example, imagine that you want to go out with your friends after work on Friday, leaving your partner alone for the evening. So to arrive at an enthusiastic agreement for that thoughtless activity, you suggest that you spend a Saturday alone so that your partner can go out with his or her friends. The problem with that arrangement is that you are agreeing to behavior that makes one of you unhappy while the other is happy, and as I've said earlier, that ultimately leads to incompatibility.

The Giver and Taker suggest those kinds of win-lose solutions because they don't understand the importance of win-win solutions. Their concept of fairness is that if you are both suffering equally, that's fair. But the Buyer's view of negotiation is that it should lead to a solution where neither of you suffers and both of you are happy.

Guideline 4

Choose the solution that meets the conditions of the Policy of Joint Agreement — mutual and enthusiastic agreement. After brainstorming, you will have come up with some good and some bad solutions. Now you need to sort through them. Good solutions are those both you and your partner consider desirable. Bad solutions, on the other hand, take only the feelings of one partner into account at the expense of the other. The best solution is the one that makes you and your partner enthusiastic.

Many problems are relatively easy to solve. You will be amazed at how quickly you can come to an enthusiastic agreement for some problems when you have decided to hold off on any action until you both agree. That's because when you know you must take each other's feelings into account, you become increasingly aware of what it will take to reach a mutual agreement. Instead of considering options that clearly are

Direct your mind to find only smart solutions.

not in your partner's best interest, you reject them immediately and begin to think of options you know would make both you and your partner happy. You will be much smarter when you direct your mind to find only smart solutions.

For example, consider the situation we mentioned above. You would like to go out with your friends after work Friday night, leaving your partner alone for the evening. Before you had agreed to the Policy of Joint Agreement, you may have simply called your partner to announce your plans or, worse yet, not called at all. But now you must come to an enthusiastic agreement prior to the event. It certainly restricts your freedom of choice, but on the other hand, it protects your partner from your thoughtless behavior.

After presenting your case, you may hear immediate objections. Your partner may feel that he or she does not appreciate being left alone while you're out having fun. "Besides," your partner may mention, "we should be with each other on Friday nights." In response, you might suggest that your partner join you.

If you and your partner can enthusiastically agree on that suggestion, you are home free. Your partner joins you and your friends. Problem solved. In fact, if going out after work Friday night with friends becomes a regular event, you can plan ahead for it by inviting your partner in advance. But if you want your partner's continuing enthusiastic agreement about such a plan, make sure your partner enjoys being with your friends as much as you enjoy it. If you neglect our partner whenever you are with your friends, his or her enthusiasm will be very short-lived.

Of course, other problems can be very difficult to solve, involving many steps. Learning how to meet each other's emotional needs, for example, can require quite a bit of trial and error, along with the time and energy it takes to create the habits that eventually make meeting a need almost effortless. If you need help, my book *His Needs, Her Needs* and its accompanying workbook *Five Steps to Romantic Love* will show you how to become experts at meeting each other's most important emotional needs.

But what can you do if you have agreed to follow the Policy of Joint Agreement, tried to negotiate for a mutually enthusiastic solution, and yet you or your partner keep behaving in a way that is objectionable to the other? This kind of thoughtless behavior may turn out to be an addiction.

If one of you struggles with an addiction, you will find that the Policy of Joint Agreement simply cannot be followed until you have overcome the addiction. Whether it's drugs, alcohol, sex, gambling, or even being with your friends on Friday night, thoughtfulness is almost impossible to practice as long as you are addicted. You must sweep the addiction completely out of your life before you will be able to negotiate in the way I have suggested.

So if you have tried to follow my advice but can't seem to negotiate with each other regardless of how hard you try, addiction may be the culprit. In fact a good way to determine if you are addicted to a substance or activity is to see if you can follow the Policy of Joint Agreement after you have agreed to it. If you find you can't, you may need professional help to overcome your addiction. But once it's overcome, the Policy of Joint Agreement will help prevent you from returning to it later.

Practice Using the Policy of Joint Agreement

If you follow the guidelines I have suggested, negotiation can be an enjoyable way to learn about each other. And if you avoid unpleasant scenes and negotiate to an enthusiastic agreement, you can resolve with relative ease all of the many conflicts you will have throughout life.

The more you practice following these guidelines, the less conflict you will experience. Once you have arrived at an enthusiastic agreement about one conflict, you will have set a precedent for whenever that situation occurs in the future. So the more conflicts you resolve with enthusiasm, the fewer conflicts you will have to resolve later.

I've given you some straightforward principles in this chapter, but you may still wonder about how all of this really

The more you practice following these guidelines,
the less conflict you will experience.

works in practice. So I encourage you to discuss the pros and cons of the Policy of Joint Agreement with your partner. You will tend to want your partner to consider your feelings when he or she makes a decision, but you may not be quite as willing to consider your partner's feelings when you make a decision. That's the Taker at work. Discuss how the Policy of Joint Agreement injects fairness into the way you try to resolve conflicts.

The main purpose of the Policy of Joint Agreement is to force you to negotiate with each other instead of making unilateral decisions. In fact, without the Policy of Joint Agreement, you may find yourselves with very little will to negotiate. Think of a few examples of recent decisions that either of you made unilaterally, and think of ways you could have made a better decision if you had been forced to use the Policy of Joint Agreement.

The Four Guidelines for Successful Negotiation sound like a very formal and difficult procedure to follow. But in practice, they can be quite easily implemented, even on the run, if you are in the habit of using them. Remember my scuba diving experience? I had to practice emergency procedures until they

Practice negotiating successfully.

were second nature to me. That way, when I was faced with a real emergency, I knew what to do. In the same way, you need to practice negotiating with each other until it becomes such a habit that you know exactly what to do when a conflict arises. So to help you get into the habit of using these four guidelines and the Policy of Joint Agreement, I suggest the following assignment to practice negotiating successfully.

Go to a grocery store together, and for about fifteen minutes select items for your cart that you are both enthusiastic about buying. This should be "pretend" buying and is only to be used for the purpose of practice. Your actual grocery purchases should be done the way you normally buy groceries. I recommend this exercise so you will have a chance to make decisions on an issue that does not have serious consequences for either of you. That way you can learn the basic steps of negotiation without having to deal with the emotional reactions that accompany real conflicts you may be having. While you are shopping together, if one of you wants an item that the other is not enthusiastic about purchasing, negotiate with your partner to try to create enthusiasm. Demands, disrespect, and anger do not work, so don't even think of using them to get what you want. And be sure you are cheerful as you discuss each item.

You will find that a test of an item's value to the reluctant partner will often have favorable results. "Try it, you'll like it," can often give your proposal a chance for enthusiastic acceptance. But if the trial fails to convince, accept defeat graciously.

Avoid making bargains that let you have one item that your partner doesn't like in exchange for your partner having an item you don't like. In many cases, if you simply cannot enthusiastically agree on an item that one of you wants, you must pass on that item. Make sure that each item is chosen with an enthusiastic agreement, or it doesn't go into the cart. Each time your fifteen minutes are up, and you don't actually want to buy the items, put them back on the shelf before you leave the store.

Repeat this exercise on several occasions until you can fill your cart with groceries in the fifteen minutes you have scheduled. When you begin the exercise, you will go right to the items that you are already mutually enthusiastic about buying, and you will add to those during the exercise. The items that were rejected earlier can be reconsidered with a new and more persuasive demonstration of their value. But remember not to put pressure on each other or use any tactic that either of you finds annoying. In fact this exercise will help you identify effective and enjoyable persuasion tactics and rule out those that are ineffective and irritating.

The eventual filling of the cart symbolizes the compatible lifestyle that you will build together by following the Policy of Joint Agreement. Life, just like the grocery store, is so full of possibilities that you can experience only a fraction of them. And among those possibilities, there are some that make neither of you happy, those that make only one of you happy and the other unhappy, and those that make both of you happy. Why build your lifestyle on anything other than choices that make both of you happy? There are so many of those win-win possibilities that you could never experience all of them anyway. And the best way to discover them is to keep looking until you find them.

The very act of asking each other how you feel regarding each item in question, and holding off on making a decision until you have agreement, is an extremely important habit to learn if you want to become compatible and be in love with each other. When you think you have the hang of it, tackle some real conflicts with the Four Guidelines to Successful Negotiation and the Policy of Joint Agreement.

As you learn to resolve your conflicts the right way, you will be doing what Buyers do. When that happens, don't be surprised if you begin thinking about eventually becoming a Buyer by making your relationship exclusive and permanent in marriage.

13

Ready to Buy?

Romantic relationships today are not at all like they were when I was dating Joyce more than forty years ago. Back then most of the men and women I knew were eagerly awaiting the day that they would be married and raise a family. I was twenty-one when I married Joyce; she was only nineteen. And Joyce was married much later than her mom, who was only sixteen when she married Joyce's dad.

Today getting married that early is often regarded as irre-sponsible. It's viewed by many as a surefire way to guarantee eventual divorce. But Joyce's parents had a terrific marriage and so do Joyce and I. That's because the age at the time of marriage is irrelevant as long as both people are Buyers. It is true, however, that the younger you are, the more likely you are to be a Freeloader or a Renter after marriage. When I was fifteen, I was definitely a Freeloader, and when I reached eighteen, I was a Renter. Thankfully, by the time I was mar-ried, I knew how to become a Buyer.

But waiting until you are thirty does not guarantee that you will be a Buyer when you marry. In fact I know many people who have never been Buyers, yet they have been married several times. Some of these people are Freeloaders. They think they have not yet found the right person because no one has been willing to put up with their thoughtless behavior.

Others are Renters, who have found that their marriages all seem to lead to abuse and suffering. They don't understand

Only Buyers know how to form exclusive
and permanent romantic relationships.

how their willingness to sacrifice and demand sacrifice in return leads to an abusive relationship. They think they are somehow drawn to abusive partners. But it's their problem-solving strategy that makes their relationships turn out to be abusive. If they were to look at themselves objectively, they would probably see that they are just as abusive as their partner.

A Freeloader doesn't have the ability to form a long-term romantic relationship with anyone because of a basic unwillingness to accommodate his or her partner. When a serious conflict arises, the Freeloader will change the relationship rather than change his or her behavior. Renters also fail to have long-term romantic relationships because of the abusive ways they approach behavioral change. If you have ever been in an abusive relationship, you and your partner were probably Renters.

Only Buyers know how to form exclusive and permanent romantic relationships. They do it by making decisions that work well for both partners. Demands, disrespect, and anger are almost unknown in those relationships, because Buyers learn to treat each other the way they would want to be treated themselves. They function as an integrated unit.

I attended a thirty-five-year high school reunion a few years ago and sat at a table surrounded by my high school friends. Others I had known well filled nearby tables. Of all the old friends I saw that evening, only one was still married to his first wife. All the others, men and women alike, had been divorced at least once.

The situation was ironic because this one friend was an unlikely prospect for the marriage-survival award. While he was enrolled in a shop course with me in the eleventh grade, his girlfriend became pregnant and he dropped out of high school to support his new family. Yet as far as I know, he's the only friend I had in high school whose first marriage is still successful. Despite his young age, he learned to be a Buyer, and that has made his marriage thrive.

Your high school friends are probably doing better in their marriages than my friends. After all, I went to high school in

He learned to be a Buyer, and that has made his marriage thrive.

California. But I'm sure that when you attend your thirty-five-year reunion, many, if not most, of your friends will have been divorced at least once. And many will have never married at all.

Are you afraid to be married because of the disasters you see around you? The kind of marriage your parents have may not be what you want, even if they have managed to remain married. And your friends' marriages might be disasters in the making. It can easily begin to appear as if marriage is a disease that eventually kills everything you want in life and leaves you with nothing.

But that's not been my experience. I wouldn't trade my marriage for anything. It has been everything I have wanted in life, and I'm not alone in my experience. My high school friend has also had the same positive experience. In fact millions of others are experiencing very fulfilling marriages.

If you could know now that you would be fulfilled in your romantic relationship thirty-five years from now, would you have enough confidence to make it exclusive and permanent? I guarantee you that outcome if you and your partner will make all your decisions the right way—with each other's interests in mind. What makes romantic relationships turn into nightmares is not some inevitable quirk of fate but rather the flawed problem-solving strategies of Freeloaders and Renters. If you replace those strategies with the successful strategy of the Buyer, your romantic relationship will be as fulfilling to both of you as you could have ever imagined.

No one is born to be a Freeloader or a Renter for life. And Buyers are not born to be Buyers either. What makes a person a Buyer, a Renter, or a Freeloader are the choices they make when they are in a romantic relationship. Fortunately Joyce and I both made the choice to be Buyers at the time of our wedding. For years, as I tried to counsel couples who were about to divorce, I didn't know what it was that made our marriage more successful than others. But now I can tell you definitively that it is the way we resolve our conflicts. We care for each other with every decision we make.

If you have been a Renter all your life, trying to survive increasingly abusive romantic relationships with other Renters, or even if you've been a Freeloader, looking for just the right partner, your future can be very different from your past. All it takes is a willingness on the part of both you and your partner to become Buyers, and that means following the Policy of Joint Agreement. It may take a while for you to get the hang of it, and some of your Renting and Freeloading friends may find your efforts laughable, since they are not Buyers and don't understand the Buyer's way of doing things. But in the end, you will have a great romantic relationship, and they will all still be struggling to find someone to love.

The entertainment industry is made up mostly of Renters and Freeloaders. There's hardly a Buyer anywhere in sight in

> *There are Buyers all around you,*
> *and you can be one too.*

Hollywood. Movies and television series all portray romantic relationships as Renters' and Freeloaders' relationships because those are the only ones they understand. And you are not too likely to get the Buyer's perspective from most professional marital therapists these days either. Many, if not most, of them are working on their second or third marriage.

But there are Buyers all around you. They are those who are affectionate with each other in public, like Joyce and I are, even after forty years of marriage. They almost never fight with each other, and they demonstrate their commitment to each other's happiness in a host of different ways. You won't see them in movies or on television, but they are a very large segment of our society. If your parents and friends are all Freeloaders and Renters and you want some exposure to Buyers, take a closer look at married couples that are obviously still in love with each other after forty years of marriage. They will tell you the same thing I've been telling you in this book. If you want to be happily married, you must do whatever makes you both happy and avoid what makes one of you unhappy. It's what makes them Buyers. And it's what can make you a Buyer too.

Appendix A

Romantic Relationship Attitudes Questionnaire

On a blank sheet of paper, write the numbers 1 through 30 to represent each question in the questionnaire. Then, beside each number, write either a T or F as your answer to that question. Use the key at the end of the questionnaire to determine your score.

1. If I am getting less than I need from _____, it's reasonable for me to expect him or her to sacrifice his or her happiness for my fulfillment.
2. Romantic relationships require a certain amount of give and take, but what I give to _____ should be worth what I take. In other words, I should be able to get out of this relationship what I put into it.
3. If we are right for each other, _____ will not want me to change.

4. I will be in an exclusive romantic relationship with _____ for life.

5. I am willing to sacrifice my happiness once in a while to satisfy _____ if he or she is willing to sacrifice his or her happiness once in a while to satisfy me.

6. I should do for _____ only whatever comes naturally to me.

7. Our romantic relationship is fatally flawed if _____ does not accept me as I am.

8. The goal of my romantic relationship with _____ is for us both to be happy and fulfilled with each other. As such, we must both learn to do everything with each other's interests and feelings in mind.

9. If _____ expects me to do something in return for his or her care of me, we are probably not right for each other.

10. If what I get in my romantic relationship with _____ isn't worth what I give, he or she should either give me more, or I should end the relationship to find someone who can give me more.

11. Solutions to the problems that _____ and I face should be long-term solutions that satisfy both of us.

12. _____ should not expect me to have a permanent romantic relationship with him or her.

13. Criticism from _____ should not cause me to try to change my behavior. It should cause me to consider ending our romantic relationship.

14. If _____ has a problem with some aspect of our romantic relationship, we should both work together to find a solution that we can permanently adopt.

15. Even though I am presently in an exclusive romantic relationship with _____, it's reasonable for me to

compare him or her to others who may meet my needs more effectively.

16. _____ and I should learn how to make each other happy without sacrificing our own happiness to do it.

17. It's reasonable for _____ to expect me to do something in return for what he or she does for me.

18. The decisions that _____ and I make should make both of us happy and fulfilled.

19. If _____ criticizes me, it means that he or she is probably not right for me.

20. A short-term sacrifice may be necessary for me to learn a new habit or create a lifestyle change that accommodates _____. But if I am not eventually happy with the habit or lifestyle change, I should not continue to make the sacrifice.

21. If _____ criticizes me, he or she simply wants me to give more to compensate for what I am taking from him or her. So it's reasonable for me to give more to him or her if I feel that he or she is giving enough to compensate me for my effort to make the change.

22. If _____ wants me to do things for him or her that I do not feel like doing, he or she is probably wrong for me.

23. The mutual enjoyment and fulfillment that _____ and I share is more important than what either of us regards as fairness.

24. _____ may be right for me now but may be wrong for me later if he or she meets my needs now but fails to meet them at a later stage of my life.

25. When my needs or those of _____ change, an adjustment in habits and lifestyle should be made by both of us to accommodate the new needs, so that our

romantic relationship can be fulfilling to both of us throughout life.

26. _____ should not expect me to have an exclusive romantic relationship with him or her.

27. My romantic relationship with _____ should last as long as I feel it is fair.

28. I should be in an exclusive romantic relationship with _____ only as long as he or she is meeting my emotional needs.

29. If _____ were critical of me, it would indicate that an adjustment of my habits and lifestyle are required until the change would satisfy him or her.

30. If _____ is right for me, he or she will make me happy without my having to put much effort into making him or her happy.

Scoring Key: Add the number of true answers for the following questions:

    4, 8, 11, 14, 16, 18, 20, 23, 25, 29:   _____
    1, 2, 5, 10, 15, 17, 21, 24, 27, 28:   _____
    3, 6, 7, 9, 12, 13, 19, 22, 26, 30:   _____

If the first group has the largest total, you are probably a Buyer. If the second group has the largest total, you are probably a Renter. And if the third group has the largest total, you are probably a Freeloader.

Share your results with your partner, referring to chapter 10 for specific suggestions on how to honestly discuss the questionnaire together.

Appendix B

Personal History Questionnaire

Answer all of the following questions as honestly and thought-fully as possible. If your answer requires additional space, use another sheet of paper.

When answering these questions, it is important to remember the Rule of Honesty and its four parts.

The Rule of Honesty for Successful Relationships

Reveal to your partner as much information about yourself as you know—your thoughts, feelings, habits, likes, dislikes, personal history, daily activities, and plans for the future.

1. *Emotional honesty:* Reveal your emotional reactions—both positive and negative—to the events of your life, particularly to your partner's behavior.

2. *Historical honesty:* Reveal information about your personal history, particularly events that demonstrate personal weakness and failure.

3. *Current honesty:* Reveal information about the events of your day. Provide your partner with a calendar of your activities, with special emphasis on those that may affect him or her.

4. *Future honesty:* Reveal your thoughts and plans regarding future activities and objectives.

I agree to consider this information confidential and will not share any information revealed in this questionnaire to anyone without my partner's permission. I also agree to reward honesty and not punish my partner for revealing any new information to me that I may find upsetting.

Signature _____ Date_____

Health History

List childhood diseases, injuries, or operations:

List past adult diseases, injuries, or operations:

List present medical problems (include high blood pressure, arthritis, migraine headaches, etc.):

When did you have your last complete physical examination?

What were the results? Did the doctor find a medical problem or are you generally in good health?

How long does it usually take you to fall asleep when you go to bed at night? _____ How many hours do you usually sleep? _____

How often do you awaken during the night? _____
How long does it take to get back to sleep? _____

How many pounds have you gained and/or lost in the past year?
_____

Describe any of your past and present diet programs:

Describe your current exercise program:

What drugs do you presently take, what dosages, how often, and for what conditions?

Have you ever been hospitalized or received therapy for a mental disorder? If so, list hospital(s) and/or therapist(s) and approximate dates:

Do you now have or have you ever had venereal disease? If so, when and what were the conditions?

For the woman: When did you have your first period? _____
Are your periods regular? _____ Are they comfortable? _____ Do they cause you to feel depressed, anxious, or irritable? _____

Family History

Mother's name: _____

age: _____ occupation: _____ education:

How did she punish you?

How did she reward you?

What behaviors did she punish?

What behaviors did she reward?

How would others describe your mother?

How would you describe your mother?

What activities did you do with your mother when you were a child?

How did you get along with your mother?

Father's name: _____

age: _____ occupation: _____ education:

How did he punish you?

How did he reward you?

What behaviors did he punish?

What behaviors did he reward?

How would others describe your father?

How would you describe your father?

What activities did you do with your father when you were a child?

How did you get along with your father?

For each of your brother(s) and sister(s), give name, birth date, and how you got along with him/her when you were growing up together:

Does (did) your mother or father favor one child? If so, who and why do you think they favored that child?

Were your mother and father divorced? If so, how old were you and what do you know about the reasons they divorced?

How do (did) your mother and father get along?

Was your father or mother (or both) an alcoholic? If so, how did it affect your childhood?

Describe any instances of physical violence or sexual advances inflicted on you by a parent or sibling when you were a child.

If you were raised by a stepparent or foster parents, please describe your most important experiences with them.

Educational History

What preschool(s) did you attend?

Describe any significant experiences there:

What elementary school(s) did you attend?

Were you a good student? _____ Describe any significant experiences at your elementary school:

What middle and/or secondary school(s) did you attend?

What were your grades? _____ Describe any significant experiences at your middle school or secondary school:

What college(s) or vocational school(s) did you attend?

What were your grades? _____ Describe any significant experiences at college or vocational school:

What was your major or specialization? _____

Give degree and date earned:

What postgraduate school(s) did you attend?

What were your grades? _____ Describe any significant experiences in postgraduate school:

What was your major?

Give degree and date earned: _____

Describe sports or other extracurricular activities in which you participated, awards you received, and musical instruments you played throughout your education.

What are your future educational plans?

Vocational History

List the jobs you have held, giving the present or most recent job first. For each job, give the dates you were employed, your job title and salary, and what you liked and disliked about the job.

How often do you miss work at jobs you enjoy?

At jobs you dislike?

Describe how well you get along with your fellow employees:

Describe how well you get along with your supervisor(s):

What training or education have you had that is relevant to your present occupation?

Does your job satisfy you intellectually? _____ emotionally? _____ physically? _____

What are your vocational ambitions?

What were your childhood interests and hobbies?

What are your present leisure time interests and hobbies?

Religious History

What is the name of your religion?

Describe your most important religious beliefs.

How do your religious beliefs influence the decisions you make in your life?

List your religious activities (prayer, study, meetings, etc.) and how frequently you participate in each one:

Describe how your religious beliefs and those of your parents affected your childhood:

Describe any differences between your religious beliefs and those of your partner:

Describe any important changes in your religious beliefs during your lifetime:

Opposite-Sex Relationship History

List all *significant* opposite-sex relationships you had prior to high school and give the person's name, your age, and the person's age during the relationship, and the duration of the relationship. Indicate if you were in love and if you had a sexual relationship (use separate sheet of paper if needed):

List all *significant* opposite-sex relationships you had during high school and give the person's name, your age, and the person's age during the relationship, and the duration of the relationship. Indicate if you were in love and if you had a sexual relationship (use separate sheet of paper if needed):

List all *significant* opposite-sex relationships you had after high school and give the person's name, your age, and the person's age during the relationship, and the duration of the relationship. Indicate if you were in love and if you had a sexual relationship (use separate sheet of paper if needed):

If you have been divorced, give the name of your former spouse, date married, date divorced, reason for divorce, what you liked most and disliked most about the person, and the names and birth dates of children (use separate sheet of paper if needed):

If you have been widowed, give the name of your spouse, date married, date and cause of spouse's death, what you liked most and disliked most about your spouse, and the names and birth dates of children (use separate sheet of paper if needed):

Sexual History

When and how did you first learn about sex?

How did your parents influence your attitude regarding sex?

What was your parents' attitude concerning sex? (circle one of the following)

1. Sex was shameful and not to be discussed.
2. Sex was not shameful but it wasn't discussed.
3. Sex was shameful but was also discussed.
4. Sex was not shameful and was freely discussed.

Describe your first sexual experience:

Describe your most important sexual experiences and how they influenced the way you think about sex today:

When and how did you first experience sexual arousal and how did you feel about it?

If you have experienced sexual climax, describe the first time. How did you feel about it?

If you have ever masturbated, when did you start?

How often did you masturbate during childhood?

During adolescence?

What sexual fantasies do you have when you masturbate?

If you have had sexual intercourse, describe the first time. How did the experience affect you?

With how many people have you had sexual intercourse? _____

Have you ever:

  had sexual experiences with or fantasies about being treated violently? _____

  had sexual experiences with or fantasies about treating others violently? _____

  exposed yourself or desired to expose yourself in public? _____

  had sexual contact with children or desired to have sexual contact with children? _____

Have you ever been in legal trouble because of your sexual behavior? If so, describe the behavior and circumstances.

Have you ever had a sexual relationship with a married person? If so, please describe the relationship(s).

Have you ever had a homosexual experience(s)? If so, please describe it.

Personal Assessment

Describe some of your fears:

Describe faults you think you have:

Describe your good characteristics:

If you ever have any of the thoughts given below, check the frequency of occurrence:

Type of thought	hardly ever	occasionally	frequently
I am lonely.	_____	_____	_____
The future is hopeless.	_____	_____	_____
Nobody cares about me.	_____	_____	_____
I feel like killing myself.	_____	_____	_____
I am a failure.	_____	_____	_____
I am intellectually inferior.	_____	_____	_____
I am going to faint.	_____	_____	_____
I am going to panic.	_____	_____	_____
People don't usually like me.	_____	_____	_____

Other negative thoughts you may have occasionally or frequently:

_____

_____

_____

Indicate the degree that the following problems are a concern to you using this scale:

X = concern in the past, not now

0 = never a concern

1 = very slight degree of concern

2 = mild degree of concern

3 = moderate degree of concern

4 = severe degree of concern

5 = very severe degree of concern

sadness _____

suicidal feelings _____

loss of energy _____

low self-esteem _____

isolation and loneliness _____

sleep disturbance _____

headaches _____

dizziness _____

angry feelings _____

mood swings _____

verbal or emotional abuse _____

physical abuse _____

sexual abuse _____

financial problems _____

career problems _____

parent/child problems _____

Goals for Personal Improvement

Below is a list of bad habits and uncomfortable feelings that may include some that are making you feel anxious and depressed. Check off any habits or uncomfortable feelings that you would like to change:

_____ drinking alcoholic beverages too much

_____ smoking too much

_____ using drugs too much—name the drug(s):

_____

_____ eating too much

_____ exercising too little

_____ feeling too much attraction to members of my own sex

_____ feeling too much attraction to members of the opposite sex

_____ feeling nauseated when nervous

_____ thinking depressing thoughts

_____ feeling anxious in crowds

_____ feeling anxious in high places

_____ worrying about my health

_____ feeling anxious in airplanes

_____ stuttering

_____ washing my hands too often

_____ cleaning and straightening things up too often

_____ biting my fingernails

_____ being careless of my physical appearance

_____ feeling anxious in enclosed places

_____ feeling anxious in open places

_____ being too afraid of blood

_____ feeling anxious about contamination or germs

_____ feeling anxious about being alone

_____ feeling afraid of darkness
_____ feeling afraid of certain animals
_____ thinking the same thoughts over and over
_____ counting my heartbeats
_____ hearing voices
_____ feeling people are against me or out to get me
_____ seeing visions or objects that aren't really there
_____ wetting the bed at night or having difficulty controlling my bladder
_____ having difficulty controlling my bowel movement
_____ taking too much medicine
_____ having too many headaches
_____ gambling too much
_____ being unable to fall asleep at night
_____ exposing my body to strangers
_____ wearing clothes of the opposite sex
_____ feeling sexually attracted to other people's clothing or belongings
_____ feeling sexually attracted to children
_____ feeling sexually attracted to animals
_____ feeling a sexual desire to hurt other people
_____ feeling a sexual desire to be hurt or humiliated
_____ feeling a nonsexual desire to hurt other people
_____ feeling a nonsexual desire to be hurt or humiliated
_____ stealing or a desire to steal
_____ lying
_____ yelling at people when I'm angry
_____ poor management of money
_____ saying foolish things to people
_____ having difficulty carrying on a conversation with people
_____ bothering or irritating people too much
_____ forgetfulness

_____ contemplating suicide
_____ setting fires or a desire to set fires
_____ difficulty being steadily employed
_____ feeling uncomfortable at work
_____ swearing
_____ being too upset when criticized by others
_____ having difficulty expressing feelings
_____ putting things off that need to be done
_____ thinking things that cause guilty feelings
_____ feeling anxious when work is being supervised
_____ feeling anxious about sexual thoughts
_____ feeling anxious about kissing
_____ feeling anxious about petting
_____ feeling anxious about sexual intercourse
_____ having difficulty making decisions when they need to be made
_____ feeling uncomfortable with groups of people
_____ feeling anxious about:
_____ feeling depressed about:
_____ feeling guilty about:
_____ being unable to control my desire to:

How do you plan to change the habits and/or uncomfortable feelings checked above?

Notes

1. Leon Festinger, *A Theory of Cognitive Dissonance* (Stanford, Calif.: Stanford University Press, 1957).

2. Bennett, Blan, and Bloom, "Commitment and the Modern Union: Assessing the Link Between Premarital Cohabitation and Subsequent Marital Stability," *American Sociological Review* 53 (1988): 127–38.

3. David Hall and John Zhao, "Cohabitation and Divorce in Canada," *Journal of Marriage and the Family* (May 1995): 421–27.

4. Alfred DeMaris and William MacDonald, "Premarital Cohabitation and Martial Instability: A Test of the Unconventionality Hypothesis," *Journal of Marriage and the Family* (May 1993): 399–407.

5. Linda J. Waite and Maggie Gallagher, *The Case for Marriage: Why Married People Are Healthier, Happier, and Better Off Financially* (New York: Broadway Books, 2000), 150–60.

Willard F. Harley, Jr. is a nationally acclaimed clinical psychologist, marriage counselor, and bestselling author. His popular website, www.marriagebuilders.com, offers practical solutions to almost any marital problem. Dr. Harley and his wife, Joyce, host a radio call-in show called *Marriage Builders Radio* as well as Marriage Builders Weekend conferences. They live in White Bear Lake, Minnesota.